Home Basics

Electrical
Made Easy

Ron Hazelton

BETTERWAY HOME
CINCINNATI, OHIO
www.popularwoodworking.com

Read This Important Safety Notice

To prevent accidents, keep safety in mind while you work. Use the safety guards installed on power equipment; they are for your protection. When working on power equipment, keep fingers away from saw blades, wear safety goggles to prevent injuries from flying wood chips and sawdust, wear hearing protection and consider installing a dust vacuum to reduce the amount of airborne sawdust in your woodshop. Don't wear loose clothing, such as neckties or shirts with loose sleeves, or jewelry, such as rings, necklaces or bracelets, when working on power equipment. Tie back long hair to prevent it from getting caught in your equipment. People who are sensitive to certain chemicals should check the chemical content of any product before using it. The authors and editors who compiled this book have tried to make the contents as accurate and correct as possible. Plans, illustrations, photographs and text have been carefully checked. All instructions, plans and projects should be carefully read, studied and understood before beginning construction. Due to the variability of local conditions, construction materials, skill levels, etc., neither the author nor Popular Woodworking Books assumes any responsibility for any accidents, injuries, damages or other losses incurred resulting from the material presented in this book. Prices listed for supplies and equipment were current at the time of publication and are subject to change.

Metric Conversion Chart

to convert	to	multiply by
Inches	Centimeters	2.54
Centimeters	Inches	0.4
Feet	Centimeters	30.5
Centimeters	Feet	0.03
Yards	Meters	0.9
Meters	Yards	1.1

HOME BASICS: ELECTRICAL MADE EASY. Copyright © 2009 by Ron Hazelton. Printed and bound in China. All rights reserved. No part of this book may be reproduced in any form or by any electronic or mechanical means including information storage and retrieval systems without permission in writing from the publisher, except by a reviewer, who may quote brief passages in a review. Published by Betterway Home, an imprint of F+W Media, Inc., 4700 East Galbraith Road, Cincinnati, Ohio, 45236. First edition.

Distributed in Canada by Fraser Direct
100 Armstrong Avenue
Georgetown, Ontario L7G 5S4
Canada

Distributed in the U.K. and Europe by David & Charles
Brunel House
Newton Abbot
Devon TQ12 4PU
England
Tel: (+44) 1626 323200
Fax: (+44) 1626 323319
E-mail: postmaster@davidandcharles.co.uk

Distributed in Australia by Capricorn Link
P.O. Box 704
Windsor, NSW 2756
Australia

Visit our Web site at www.popularwoodworking.com.

Other fine Popular Woodworking Books are available from your local bookstore or direct from the publisher.

13   12   11   10   09   5   4   3   2   1

Library of Congress Cataloging-in-Publication Data

Hazelton, Ron.
  Home basics. Electrical / by Ron Hazelton.
      p. cm.
  Includes bibliographical references and index.
  ISBN 978-1-55870-896-9 (pbk. : alk. paper)
  1. Electric engineering–Amateurs' manuals. I. Title. II. Title: Electrical.
  TK9901.H38 2009
  621.319'24–dc22
                                        2009006720

Acquisitions Editor: David Thiel
Senior Editor: Jim Stack
Designers: Brian Roeth and Doug Mayfield
Production Coordinator: Mark Griffin

About the Author

Ron Hazelton is a leading authority in the do-it-yourself home improvement field and is the host of "Ron Hazelton's HouseCalls", a nationally syndicated home improvement television show in its tenth season. He served as the Home Improvement Editor for ABC's Good Morning America, and created, co-produced and hosted "The House Doctor", a series that aired on the Home and Garden Television Network (HGTV) for over five years. He hosted the History Channel series, "Hands on History," and other History Channel programs including, "Modern Marvels" and "Save our History: Frontier Homes." Ron has also offered his home improvement expertise on "The Oprah Winfrey Show" and "Inside Edition" and is the author of *Ron Hazelton's HouseCalls: America's Most Requested Home Improvement Projects.* He operates the web site www.ronhazelton.com and publishes a weekly online newsletter.

Acknowledgements

For Danielle, Max and Lynn who have improved our home more than I could ever have imagined.

CONTENTS

● SECTION ONE: **POWER** ● SECTION TWO: **LIGHTING**

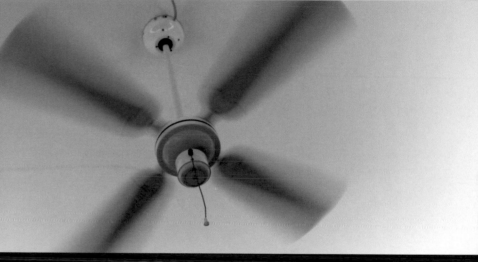

● SECTION THREE: **OUTDOOR**   ● SECTION FOUR **... AND MORE**

INTRODUCTION

If you're reading this book it's most likely because you've decided to take matters into your own hands. For that, I commend you.

I've been a do-it-yourselfer most of my life thanks to a dad who introduced me to tools and the workshop even before I headed off to kindergarten. I am lucky to have had parents who encouraged me to work and learn with my hands. Perhaps, because learning how to do things myself so enriched my life, I have spent the past decade-and-a-half sharing with others many of my hands-on adventures.

What I've noticed is that folks of any age and with any amount of previous experience can get really good at doing it themselves. Only two things are required — a desire to learn and the willingness to jump in and give it a try. In fact, gaining knowledge, solving problems and building how-to skills can be downright fun.

And what's the end result of all this? Improvements to our homes that we get to live with and enjoy day-in and day-out and the confidence and competence that comes from knowing what's behind the walls that surround us and how those things work.

Doing-it-ourselves doesn't mean doing it all alone. There's a lot of help out there in the form of books, magazines, television shows and internet sites. I hope you find *Home Basics Electrical Made Easy* to be a valuable addition to those resources.

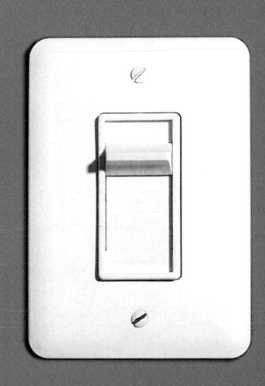

SAFETY & TOOLS

SAFETY

Safety in electrical home improvement projects should always be a first consideration. While the projects we're working on (fixing a lamp, adding a dimmer switch) all concern items that we work with in our home on a daily basis — getting close to the power that makes these conveniences work can be hazardous.

We all know the relative or neighbor who says he or she doesn't need to shut off the power to work on a switch or outlet. "It's only a little tickle." So what! It's 110 volts of electricity coursing through your body. Find the fuse or breaker and turn it off. It will allow you to work with confidence and comfort around your project.

And while you're at it, take a moment to label the fuse or breaker if it's not already labelled. It will save you time and anxiety during your next project.

I mentioned 110 volt power. That's not the only power in your house. 220 volt is used to power the larger appliances in your house, including your clothes dryer, stove and heating and air conditioning systems. This book is designed as detailed, helpful instruction for the most basic of home electrical projects. Because

of that, we've not included any projects that involve 220-volt power. You should be aware, however, that in some instances 220 volt could be run through your house and divided into 110-volt applications. This is an excellent argument for "throwing the breaker", even if you think it's fine.

In a number of the projects included in this book, we've shown not only the straightforward project, but often some of the complications that can occur during a "simple" project. In these instances we've shown how to fix the complication, and these fixes can require the use of tools not normally associated with electrical work (see the tool section following this). These tools include saws and in some cases propane torches. If at any time in any of these projects you feel uncomfortable with your confidence in using the tool, or performing the task we hope that you will listen to your instincts and know that it's time to consult a professional. There's no shame associated with this instinct, it's a survival instinct, and one that I will always respect.

Tools for working with electrical projects include the simple screwdriver, voltage testers and ladders. While I talk a bit more about screwdrivers for working with electricity on the following pages, you shouldn't overlook the obvious (and not so obvious) safety concerns when using even a ladder. If you're climbing a ladder with your hands full of tools, gravity is not your friend. Be smart.

Speaking of voltage testers, I can't emphasize enough the value of these tools (whether simple or advanced). These are relatively inexpensive tools that will provide peace of mind, and can save your life.

Which leads me to another electrical concern. Some electrical projects happen in wet places — kitchens,

and baths, for example. Electricity and water don't mix, so be extra cautious when these two enter together in your project.

While there are certainly safety issues specifically related to working around electricity, don't overlook the basic safety concepts either. Safety glasses, safety gloves and dust masks can all be beneficial when working under cabinetry and around insulation.

Finally, while all but a couple of the projects in this book can be accomplished with only one person, it's always a better idea to have someone handy. Whether it's to hand you a needed tool while you're in an awkward space, or just to be there in case, the buddy system is still an excellent idea when working with home projects, and electricity.

TOOLS

Happily, most of the tools you'll use in home electrical projects are likely already in your tool box. Some basics include: a hammer; a drill (cordless or corded) with standard drill bits; a flashlight (seems when you throw the breaker on an outlet, the lights sometimes go out, too); and a ladder for some of the ceiling projects.

Some specialty tools that will make life easier during your electrical projects (and you may already have these as well) are shown here.

Screwdrivers

Electrical work will likely require both a straight (top) and Phillips screwdriver. While you may already have these tools at home, the ones shown here are insulated to protect against accidental shock while working on electrical projects.

Voltage Tester

Whether it's the simplest version (around $3) shown here, or a more sophisticated version, it's very smart to have one of these tools handy before you go very far into your electrical project. For more on this handy tool, see the story on page 14.

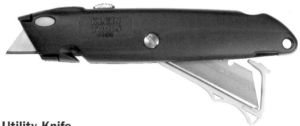

Utility Knife

You end up cutting a lot of wire when working with electricity. Whether cutting for length, or stripping the outer insulation from a wire, a basic (I prefer retractable) utility knife is an important part of your electrical tool kit.

Pliers

Used for getting a better grip on wires in tight places, and also to make those tricky loops on the ends of the wire (to attach to an outlet or switch) I prefer a pair of needle-nose pliers. They also come in handy removing the metal knock-out discs in power boxes. Conveniently the ones shown at left also include a wire cutter!

 #22 to #16 gauge

 #22 to #14 gauge

Wire Strippers

Once the wires are cut to length, you need to strip the insulation off to reach bare wire. A decent wire stripper will save a lot of frustration, and nicked fingers.

 #22 to #14 gauge

Fish Wire

A stiff, flat metal wire with a hook, if you're pulling wire through a wall, this is a tool you'll need, and love.

 #18 to #12 gauge

 **#18 to #10 gauge**

Electrical Tape

Used to connect and insulate bare wires, this tape should be used in addition with wire nuts.

Wire Nuts

Designated by color to match specific wire gauges, these connect and protect a wire connection.

SECTION ONE

Power

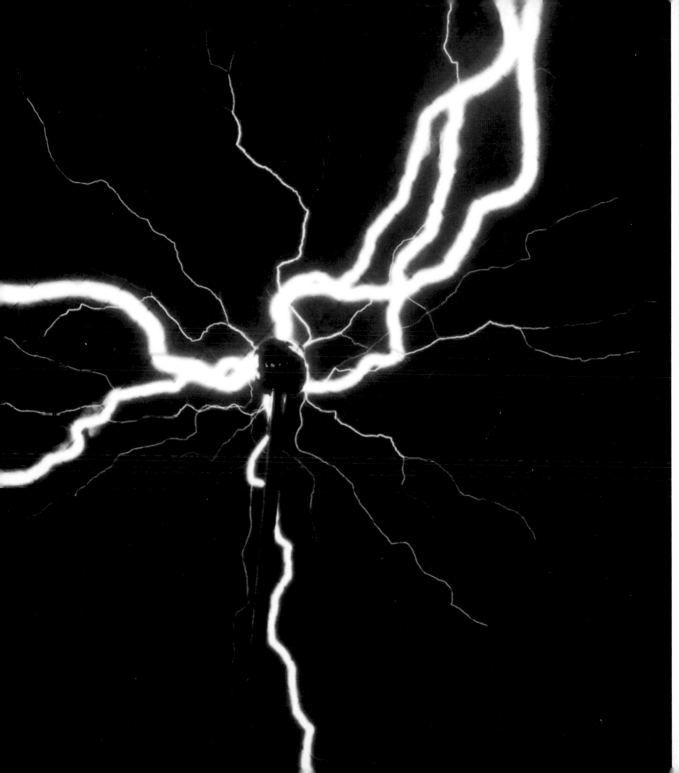

Working with Electrical Testers

MORE THAN JUST FOR SAFETY, TESTERS PROVIDE A LEVEL OF CONVENIENCE AND CONFIDENCE DURING ANY ELECTRICAL TASK.

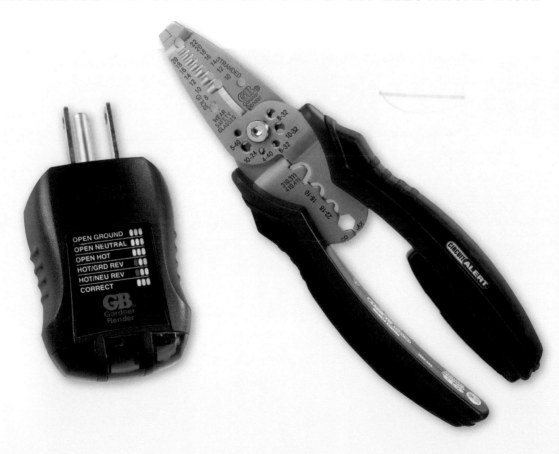

1 There are a whole bunch of cool testers to help you keep your electrical project safe. Let me show you just a few.

2 This low-cost voltage tester has two probes that can be inserted into the slots of a receptacle.

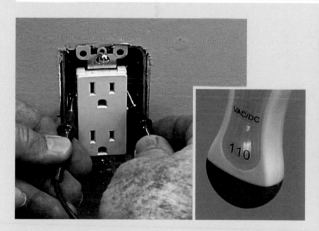

3 Is the receptacle still hot? It appears so.

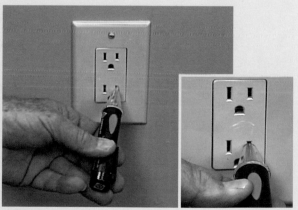

4 This pen-style detector has an audible and visual signal, and a single probe. Unlike the pigtail probe (above and at left), it requires no direct contact ...

5 ... and can sense electrical flow, even through a wire's insulation.

6 Some electrical tools, like this wire stripper, have built-in detectors ...

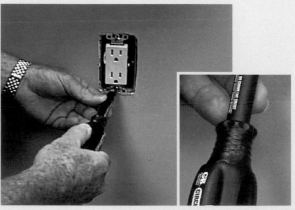

7 ... in this case, in the handle, giving both an audible and visible warning that the electrical line is live.

8 This screwdriver alerts the user, with both an audible and visible signal, that current is still flowing.

9 A plug-in circuit detector, like this one, not only detects current, but also lets you know if the outlet is wired correctly.

10 With devices like these, it's easier than ever to work safely and accurately. Make sure there's one in your electrical toolbox.

Adding a New Outlet or Switch

ADDING A SWITCH OR OUTLET MAY BE AS EASY AS REWIRING AN UNUSED PHONE JACK.

If you live in an older home, electronics and lighting get upgraded fairly often. Sometimes, what is old can be re-used for something new. Like taking a defunct phone jack and converting it into a switch for some new lighting in the kitchen.

1 This is an old telephone junction box that I don't use anymore, so I'm going to take advantage of this location and install a switch for undercabinet lighting there.

2 Step one is to remove the existing telephone jack by first removing the screws holding the cover plate in place ...

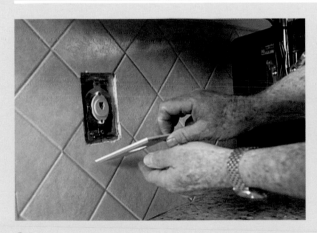

3 ... then removing the cover plate to expose the telephone jack inside.

4 Next, remove the screws that hold the jack in place.

5 Now I can just pull the assembly from the box ...

6 ... and clip off the wires.

7 Finally, I take out the box. The challenge that confronts me is to thread an electrical wire from the basement up to this opening. I'm going to do that by drilling a hole on the inside of the bottom of this wall down in the basement.

8 The question is, where do I drill that hole so that it will line up with this opening? First of all, I'll measure from the center of that opening to the edge of this casing. That's about twenty-six and a half inches.

9 Then I'll come down here and measure over the same amount (twenty-six and a half) and make a mark.

10 Next, I remove the shoe moulding at the bottom of the baseboard.

11 Then, using a long-shaft, quarter-inch drill bit, I begin boring a hole through the floor at an angle.

12 I exit at a point in the basement that's directly below the center of the wall cavity.

13 Before removing the bit, I mark the exit location, then go back upstairs and back out the drill.

14 Now, using what's called a bell-hanger's bit, I bore a larger three-quarter inch hole up into the hollow part of the wall.

15 Next, I insert the end of a stiff wire, called a fish tape, into the hole I've just drilled and push it up inside the wall.

16 Now if I've drilled at the right place, the tape should end up very close to the box opening. I continue pulling the fish tape through ...

17 ... until just a short length is left in the basement.

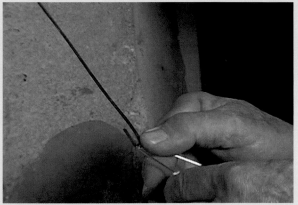

18 To that end, I attach an electrical cable ...

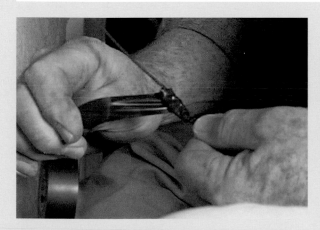

19 ... and wrap tape tightly around the connection.

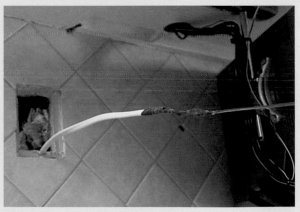

20 Then I head back upstairs and begin pulling on the fish tape, drawing the attached cable from the basement up into the kitchen.

21 I cut the tape and cable apart, then go back downstairs to connect into an existing power supply.

22 I uncoil a few more feet of wire and snip it off. Then I use a right-angle drill and auger bit to bore a series of holes through the floor joists. Keep any holes in joists centered on the width to avoid weakening the joists' support strength.

23 Then I can run the cable perpendicular to the joists, and at the same time, keep it up high and out of the way.

24 This junction box houses an electrical line that supplies power to my garbage disposal. I'll borrow some electricity from here.

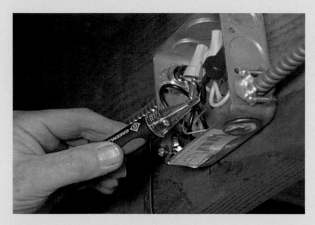

25 My voltage tester confirms it's an active circuit.

26 After flipping off the breaker, I test again to make sure the line is deactivated.

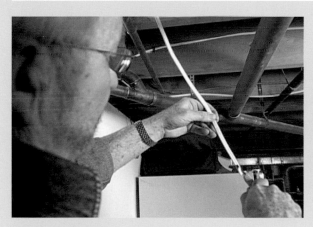

27 Next, I slice down the center of the cable to split the outer protective plastic, being careful to avoid cutting into the wires inside.

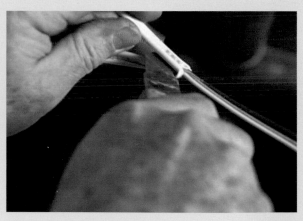

28 After peeling back the outer layer, I cut off about six inches with a utility knife.

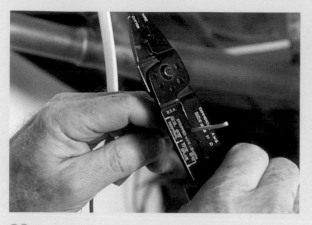

29 I then use my wire strippers to strip off the wire insulation, an inch or two from the end of each wire.

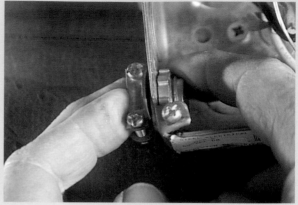

30 To keep the wires in place in the box (and up to code) I install a connector in the existing junction box ...

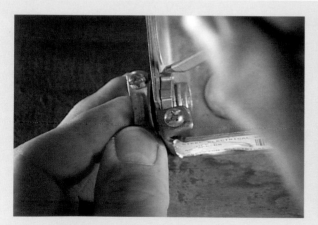

31 ... then snug up the lock nut on the inside of the box using the tip of a straight screwdriver.

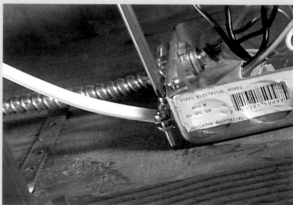

32 I then pass the wires through and tighten the connector clamp that secures the cable to the box.

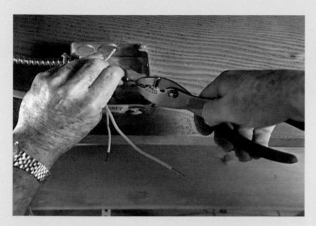

33 To connect into this circuit, all I need to do is twist together wires of the same color. Black-to-black, white-to-white and green-to-green.

34 And finally screw on the wire nuts.

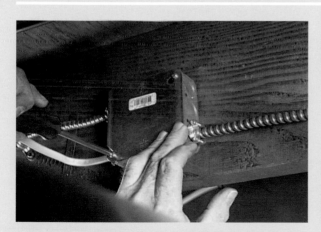

35 All that's left to do down here is replace the box cover ...

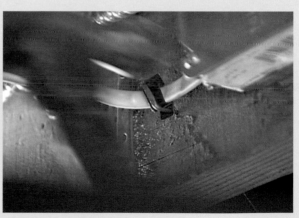

36 ... and drive in a few cable staples.

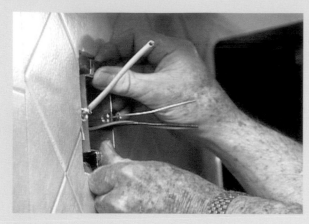

37 Unlike electrical boxes used in new construction, this box does not have to be attached to the framing.

38 Instead, it's held in place by wings that expand outward as screws on the front are tightened (right). In effect, the box is clamped front and back to the wall material, in this case, wallboard.

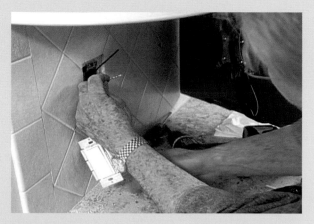

39 To install the switch, strip the insulation off the wire ends and twist the like-color wires together (three of each — from the power, the switch and the light being wired) and secure them with a wire nut.

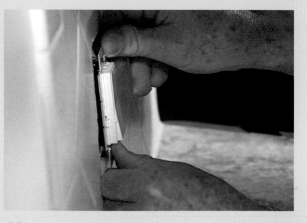

40 Now I set the switch into the box ...

41 ... secure it in place with mounting screws, place the cover plate in position and install the screws.

42 And that's all there is to turning an unused phone jack into a useful (and attractive) lighting switch. You could just as easily have installed an outlet using the same techniques.

Moving an Outlet or Switch

A FIX WHEN YOUR SWITCH OR OUTLET IS IN THE WRONG PLACE BY JUST A FEW INCHES.

I decided to upgrade the look of an open doorway leading into my living room by adding a detailed curved archway moulding to the doorway. After removing the existing trim, I realized that my light switches in the hallway would be in the way of the new moulding. Though a little more than a basic fix, moving the switch was actually a lot easier than you might think!

1 Here you see my problem. The switches will prevent the archway column from slipping into place. The solution is to move them a couple of inches to the left.

2 The first step is to remove the cover plates to expose the switches and the electrical connections.

3 After making sure that the electrical breakers for the switches are turned off (using a voltage tester to make sure), I remove the screws holding the switches to the electrical box.

4 Next I pull the switches out of the box and disconnect the wiring from the switches.

POWER

5 I then begin cutting away the wallboard so I can gain access to the wiring.

6 I carefully pry up the wallboard, pulling it free from any nails holding it in place, while making sure to do as little damage to the surrounding wallboard as possible.

7 Next, I remove the staples holding the armored cable in place.

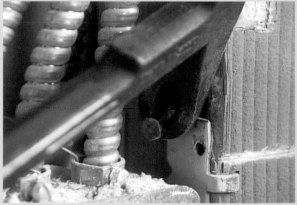

8 To remove the box, I pry the electrical box bracket free from the wall stud.

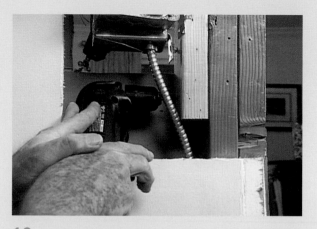

9 What I'm hoping to do is screw a two-by-four to the stud and attach a one-by-four on top, then remount the box. There's enough slack in the cable; so I can do it.

10 The two-by-four is first. A right angle drill with a screw-bit attachment lets me get into the tight space between studs. If that's not an option for you, the screws can be driven in at an angle.

11 Even with the right-angle drill, I could only use a short screw tip in the drill because of the tight space.

12 With the two-by-four in place, I next slip the one-by-four in place and attach it with a couple more screws.

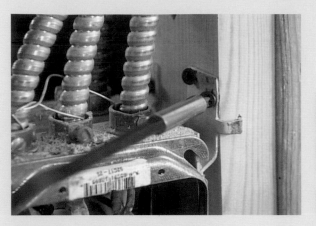

13 I then put the switch box into place and reattach it to the one-by-four with screws.

14 Now it's time to replace the wallboard. First, I attach cleats or backer boards to the inside of the wallboard.

15 The cleats span the joint between the old and new wallboard, so they are mounted with only half the width behind the old wallboard. I attach cleats at the left, and also at the top and bottom of the hole.

16 With the cleats in place, I cut the patch to fit the hole. Then using 80-grit sandpaper, I create a small bevel around the opening and on the edge of the patch. This beveling technique will allow me to make a completely flush repair without the need for tape.

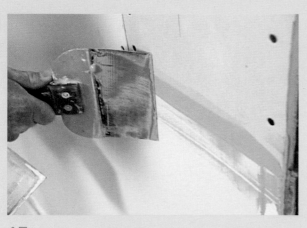

17 Finally, I simply apply the compound, press it firmly into the joint and over the recessed screw heads, then skim off the excess. I'll let this dry and do a light sanding and probably come back with a second coat. With the switch and cover plate re-installed and the trim in place, you'll never know I was inside that wall.

Tool Talk

Angled drills have been around for a number of years, and have been a popular method for working between studs. A new breed of cordless drills with vastly improved battery technology are now offering another option. These drills pack the power to sink a three-inch screw, but are small enough to fit comfortably in a pocket — or between wall studs!

Installing a GFCI Outlet

ANY PLACE THAT WATER IS FOUND, THIS IS THE OUTLET THAT WILL KEEP YOU SAFE!

Ground Fault Circuit Interrupter (GFCI) receptacles came into common use in the early 1980s. Chances are, if you're in an older home, these receptacles aren't a common sight. But for your safety, they should be. Here's how to easily upgrade your outlets.

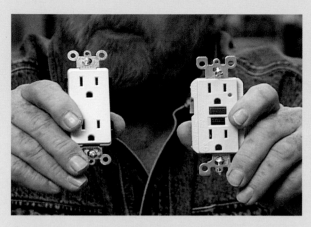

1 These are both household receptacles, but with a big difference. The one on the right is a GFCI receptacle. It's designed to protect you from an electrical shock if an appliance or tool you're using malfunctions.

2 The way it does that is to monitor the electricity going to that appliance. If there's any change to indicate that electricity is leaking from that appliance, it shuts down the circuit in a fraction of a second.

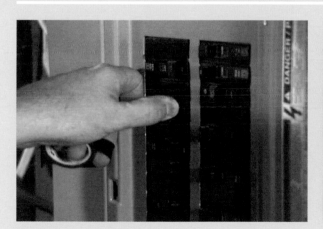

3 To install a GFCI receptacle, first turn off the power at the circuit breaker or fuse box.

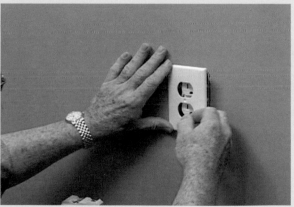

4 Then remove the cover plate ...

5 ... then back out the screws holding the old receptacle in place in the box.

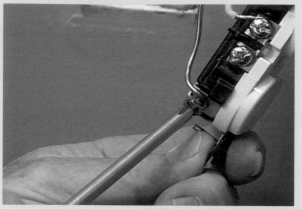

6 Carefully pull the receptacle out of the box, stretching the wires to allow convenient access. Then disconnect the wires from the receptacle.

7 Disconnect all the wires, then get your new GFCI receptacle.

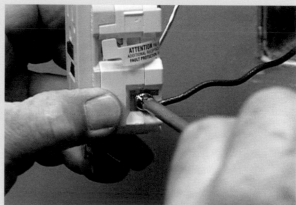

8 First connect the hot wire (it's usually black) to the gold terminal on the GFCI.

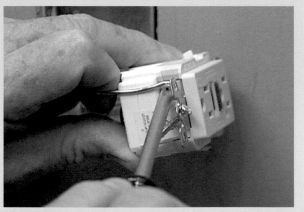

9 Then attach the white, or neutral, wire to the silver terminal.

10 And finally, connect the ground wire (usually green, or bare as it is here) to the green terminal.

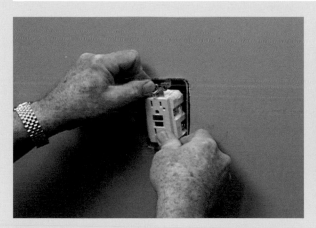

11 Gently push the receptacle back into the box. Reinstall the outlet screws, reattach the outlet plate and you're finished.

12 You want to install a GFCI outlet any place there's water and electricity. Bathrooms, kitchens, basements or outdoors. They could save your life!

Adding a Wireless Outlet

THE LAMP IS WHERE YOU WANT IT, BUT THE SWITCH ISN'T CONVENIENT — MOVE IT WITHOUT STRIPPING A WIRE!

It may be possible to build a house that meets all your lighting and switching needs. But if you're in an existing house, this little trick will let you relocate light switches without any electrical knowledge!

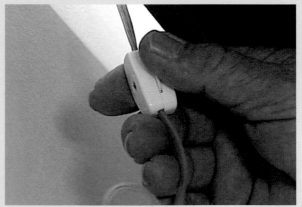

1 Every evening when the sun goes down and every night when I go to bed, I go through the same ritual with this lamp.

2 I get down on my knees, reach up underneath and turn the switch on or off because the switch is on the cord. You know what, I'm ready for a new ritual. I want a wall switch.

3 The solution for me is a wall switch that's a transmitter and a plug-in receptacle that's a receiver. These communicate with each other, not through a wire, but using wireless technology.

4 To mount the switch, I drill a couple of holes ...

5 ... insert two plastic anchors ...

6 ... attach the switch with a couple of screws ...

7 ... snap in the battery and screw on the cover. Elapsed time? About three minutes.

8 Next, I plug the lamp cord into the receiver ...

9 and plug it into the receptacle.

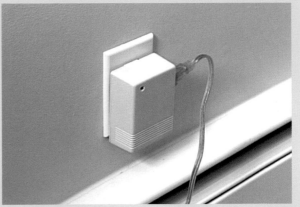

10 That's it!

11 Well how about that, all the convenience of a switch-operated outlet ...

12 ... without the hassle or expense of wiring one.

SECTION TWO

Lighting

Compact Fluorescent Lights

**SAVE MONEY, ENERGY AND THE ENVIRONMENT
BY USING COMPACT FLUORESCENT BULBS.**

The energy and cost-savings story on compact fluorescent bulbs is quite impressive. They use about one-quarter as much electricity as a conventional incandescent bulb — and they can last up to ten times as long!

1 In other words, you would have to purchase thirteen standard incandescent bulbs to equal one compact fluorescent.

2 Some folks have said to me that they object to compact fluorescent lights because of the color. But that technology has gotten a whole lot better. Now they're available in three colors ...

3 ... soft white for bedrooms and living rooms ...

4 .... bright white for bathrooms and kitchens ...

5 ... and daylight for reading or any time you want to see fine details.

6 Compact fluorescent lights used to come in only one shape, but all that's changed.

7 These covered versions look much like any other bulb.

8 Gone too are the days when compact fluorescent lights flickered to life.

9 Today's versions come on instantly.

If every American home replaced just one incandescent bulb with an EnergyStar-qualified compact fluorescent bulb we'd save enough energy to light two-and-a-half million homes for an entire year.

So just how much can a compact fluorescent bulb save you? Well, over its lifetime, which is 10,000 hours, this one-hundred watt bulb could save between $80 and $150 when compared to standard incandescent bulbs.

Replacing a Light Fixture

REPLACING AN OLD LIGHT FIXTURE CAN CHANGE THE LOOK OF A WHOLE ROOM — AND IT'S FAIRLY EASY TO DO.

Me: *It's not that bad. It's kind of Tuscanesque — a classic.*

Lynn: *I really, really hate it. How about we take down this timeless classic and try another timeless classic.*

Me: *It's like an old friend.*

Lynn: *I'll get you another friend ...*

1 We've all had these conversations. And while *my* project list calls for a chisel and the smell of wood, my wife's list has our kitchen light right at the top.

2 The first thing I do is go down to the basement and trip the circuit breaker on the light.

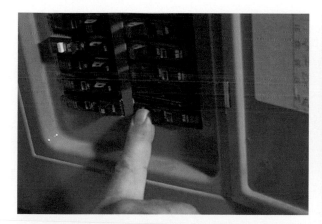

3 Just turning off the light switch can still leave power at the fixture. I always feel better if I turn the power off at the circuit breaker.

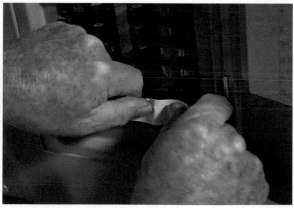

4 A piece of tape across the breaker makes sure the switch isn't accidentally turned back on.

5 Taking down the old fixture is a fairly simple job.

6 All I've really got to do is take off this canopy ...

7 ... expose the electrical box underneath, and then cut the wires. That's when I run into a problem making this project less simple. There's supposed to be an electrical box right up here that would be attached to a ceiling joist or a piece of bracing.

8 Instead, this bracket is held to the ceiling with just these two small plastic anchors — and the entire weight of that fixture was being borne by these!

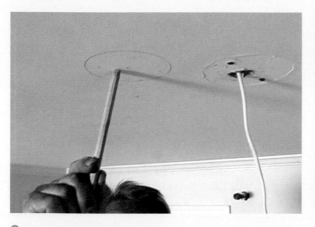

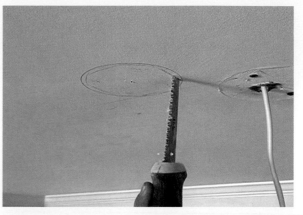

9 I'm going to move the light fixture from here, over to here, because I want to get the dining table a little bit further away from the walls. I trace around the actual box to give me the size and location of my hole.

10 I'm using my drywall saw to cut the opening for the new box location.

Tool Talk

A drywall saw (also known as a keyhole saw, plunge saw or hole saw) is a thin, tapering tool with aggressive teeth designed to cut quickly through thicker material, and still be able to turn in a tight radius during the cut. In addition, theses saws have a sharp point, allowing them to be driven into the material with a blow (from your palm, or a hammer) without the need of a starter hole. If you're doing drywall, you'll find one of these inexpensive tools valuable!

11 Now we've got to find a way to attach this box securely. I've got a special bracket for that.

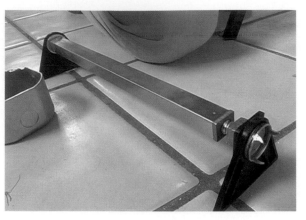

12 This is the bracket that's going to keep that box secure and support the weight of the chandelier.

13 The best way for me to explain how the bracket works is to use a mock up of what the ceiling is like. Imagine that we're looking at the ceiling from below. The bracket is fed up into the hole like this.

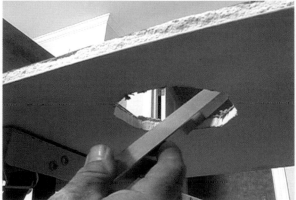

14 First one end is fed into place, then the rest of the bracket goes up through the hole until the entire bracket is in the space between two floor/ceiling joists.

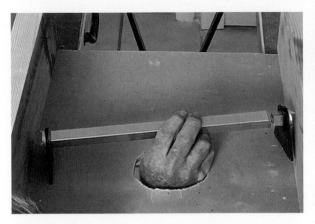

15 You reach up through the hole, like this, to position the bracket. Once it's in position ...

16 ... I rotate the bar, and as I do this, the ends of this bracket expand outward. There are some very sharp pointed ends that are now beginning to dig into the side of the ceiling joist.

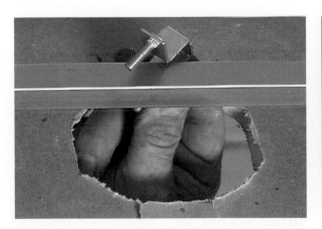

17 Next I insert this hanging bracket through the hole and up and over the bar that we put in earlier.

18 With the help of a special camera, we can look up inside the ceiling and see how the mounting and hanging brackets appear after they are in place.

19 With the bracket in place in the ceiling, I feed the wire down through the box and then slide the box in place.

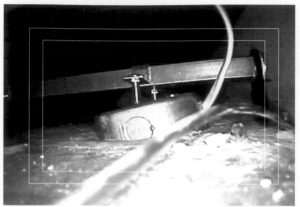

20 I wish I had a camera like this for every installation! The box has to slip over the two mounting bolts on the mounting bracket ...

21 ... and is then slid in place up against the bracket and fastened with two nuts.

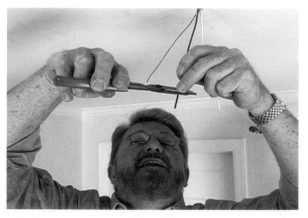

22 The wiring is basic: The hot wire here is the black one. Common, or neutral, is the white one. We've got them all separated and free of the outer covering, so now I'm just going to strip off the insulation and give myself an inch of exposed wire.

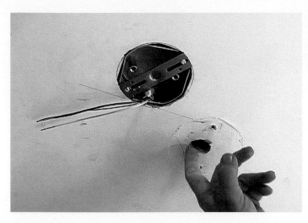

23 Before we go any farther, I want to take care of this big hole.

24 This is a strip of wood I've drilled a couple of holes through and now I'm going to put a little glue on one face.

25 Now I'll take a piece of wire — this is the one that we cut off of the wire that was sticking out of the ceiling — make a U-shape with the wire and run it through the block till the "U" stops against the block.

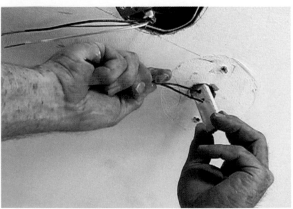

26 Next we'll push the piece of wood up inside, just like we did with the bracket earlier, and pull down on it with the glue side against the drywall.

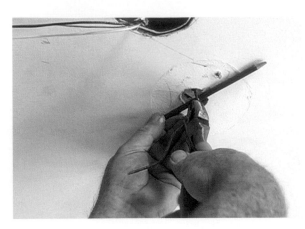

27 I want to apply a little pressure here while the glue dries, so I'm using pliers to twist the ends of the wire snugly against the pencil.

28 For shallow repairs I could use spackle. But for a deep hole like this I'm going to use a setting joint compound. It sets up quickly (fifteen to forty-five minutes). Once it's dry, I'll sand and paint.

29 Many ceiling fixtures can be heavy and awkward, so I've made a temporary hook out of a piece of hanger. I'm going to hang the chandelier on this so I don't have to hold onto it.

30 The first thing I want to do is pass these wires through this threaded nipple, like this.

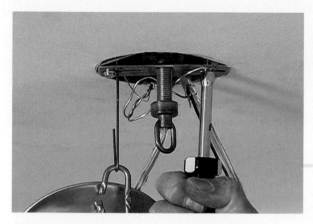

31 I'm going to feed the wires up through the bracket, and then back down. Now, we'll make our wiring connections.

32 This is our bare ground wire. Bring it around the grounding screw so the wire attaches to the fixture. This will also attach it to the strap and to the box.

33 All I have to do now is make a connection between the wires coming out of the ceiling and the ones going into the lamp, fold them and put them up inside, put the canopy up and attach the retaining ring.

34 Lynn's reaction to the working light is all I could hope for. But, I'm not done playing — I think this light needs a dimmer. Another new project!

Overhead Incandescent

**STEP-BY-STEP INSTRUCTIONS FOR REPLACING
AN OUTDATED CEILING FIXTURE.**

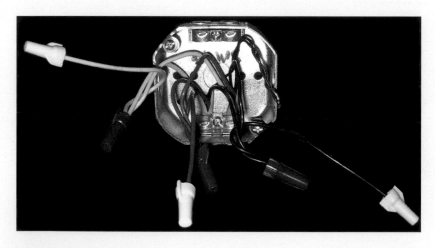

If you've never worked on the inside of an electrical box, it can be intimidating. But, with help from a friend, hanging a ceiling fixture doesn't have to be scary.

1 I'm in Monument Beach, Massachusetts with Pam McClung. She has a lighting project in her 1800's-era house that she'd like a hand with. She wants to upgrade her incandescent ceiling fixture that hangs over the dining table. It's her first electrical project and I'm here to help her through the steps.

2 First, we've got to make sure that the power is off before we start working. You might think we could just throw the wall switch, and indeed, the light will go out. But it's still possible to have electricity up there. So we want to go to the circuit breaker or fuse box and turn the power off there — at the source.

3 Here we are at the panel, and to determine which switch is for our ceiling light, we can check the labels. But to make sure, I'm going to go upstairs and let Pam throw breakers until I see the light go off.

4 With the breaker found and switched off, I've taken the globe off the fixture. Just to make sure, I'm having Pam use this tester to confirm that the power is off.

5 The same tester can be used to check for electrical current at outlets around the house.

6 To take the fixture down, Pam grabs the tube with her left hand, then reaches up above with her right hand to unscrew the fastening ring at the top of the post. You may have to wiggle it a little bit to get it loose.

7 Keep going until the cone drops down.

8 Pam touches the tester to all the wires, once again confirming that there's no current.

9 Most lights are connected with either two or three wires. The third is a ground wire. In many older houses, you may not find a ground wire connected. In this case we have all three.

10 First of all, let's disconnect the wire nuts.

11 The wires are kind of twisted together, so we'll untwist them and pull them apart.

12 This particular fixture is held up here on a threaded rod — which we'll just turn and the whole thing will come down. That's the end of the old fixture.

13 We screw the wire nuts temporarily in place on the ends of the wires.

14 Next, Pam removes the two screws that are holding the old mounting strap, or bracket, in place.

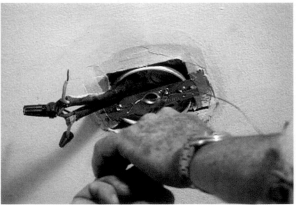

15 I've replaced the old mounting strap with a new one that was packaged with the new fixture. I'll also attach a new copper ground wire to the mounting strap.

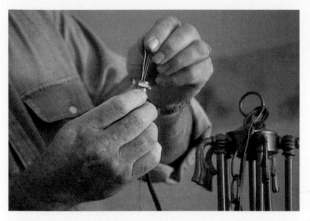

16 Now we're ready to start wiring this up. First we thread the wires through this trim plate, and then through this threaded nipple.

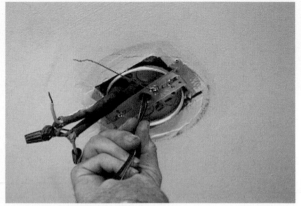

17 Next, we push the ends through the hole in the bracket and then feed them down out of the box.

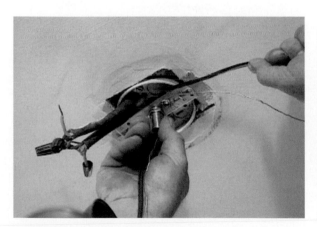

18 We screw the threaded nipple into the hole in the center of the plate or mounting bracket,

19 Now, it's time to make our connections. We connect the electrical supply wires on the new fixture to the wires coming from the ceiling box by twisting them together and screwing on insulated wire nuts.

20 Wire nuts come in different sizes, indicated by their color. The red size is what we need for this job. Green wire nuts are used here to indicate ground wires.

21 Pam secures the trim plate to the ceiling using a decorative screw eye that attaches to the threaded nipple in the mounting strap.

22 Then, she hooks an open chain link into the eye, attaches the rest of the chain to the open link, and voila — the new fixture is up.

23 The final touches are to fit the large center globe in place in the fixture ...

24 ... and to slip the four individual glass covers on the outer fixture mounts and add the decorative metallic rings.

25 The fixture is up and looking good. A quick trip back to the breaker box to throw the switch ...

26 ... and Pam's first electrical project is complete!

Overhead Fluorescent

FLUORESCENT BULBS PROVIDE MORE LIGHT, CONSUME LESS ELECTRICITY AND LAST LONGER THAN INCANDESCENT BULBS.

I'm visiting Kimberly Bower at her home in Washington state. One of the things she loves about her kitchen is that she can stand at the sink and watch eagles soaring over the water. What she doesn't like is the lighting. It's a relic from the past. So, I've agreed to help her brighten things up with some new fixtures.

1 To help Kim with her lighting issues, I'm going to help her replace her 1960's era light fixtures with new fluorescent fixtures.

2 When working with electricity, the first thing we want to do is turn off the power at the circuit breaker.

3 With the power off, I ask Kim to unscrew that round center nut at the base of the existing fixture.

4 With just a few turns the fixture is loose and we're able to get at the wiring.

5 I direct Kim to pull the wiring loose from the box ...

6 ... and remove the two red wire nuts from the wires coming out of the ceiling. With the nuts off, the fixture can be pulled down and loose.

7 The new light fixture is a T2 fluorescent. The first thing that I want to do is take out this small disk. This is the space where the wires are going to come through.

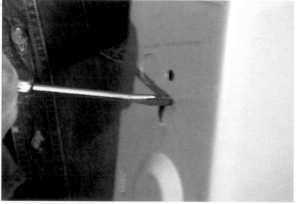

8 To remove the disk, I use a screwdriver and knock the disk loose with a tap on the screwdriver. You can use your hand or a hammer.

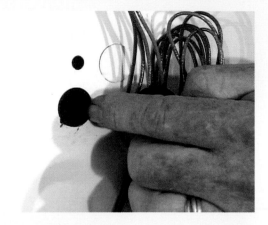

9 The disk will still be attached by a small bit of metal left uncut in the manufacturing process. I hand Kim the pliers and she gives it a twist, back and forth and it pops right out.

10 The hole left by removing the disk has pretty sharp edges that could damage the wiring. One way to fix this would be to file the edges, but I've got a better solution.

11 This rubber grommet protects the wire's insulation from fraying on the sharp edges. It slips into the hole and cushions the edges.

12 Together, Kim and I feed the wires through the grommet and hold the light fixture in place against the ceiling to mark the screw locations.

13 I use an awl to mark the ceiling through the fixtures mounting holes.

14 This is where we're supposed to drill holes for toggle bolts but we have a problem. It turns out rather than the tiles being glued to drywall, there's a space up here of almost six or seven inches. So, there's no way I can use a toggle bolt to attach the fixture here.

15 What I'm going to have to do is find some wood up here. When they put this ceiling up they used firring strips, like this, on top of the ceiling joists. There's going to be one in every joint, so what we're going to do is move the holes in the fixture, line them up with the joint and attach the fixture with wood screws.

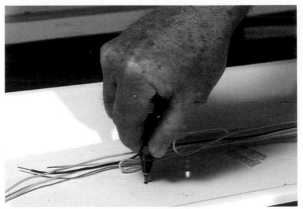

16 We need to move the mounting hole down nine inches. After measuring over from the original hole to where the joint between the tiles and the wood firing strips would be, I use a spring loaded center punch to create an indentation that will keep the drill bit from sliding.

17 Then I turn the power tools over to Kim to drill new mounting holes in the fixture.

18 Finally, we're ready to attach the fixture to the firring strips. I put the first screw in and then hand the screw gun to Kim to attach the other end.

19 Now, it's time to do some wiring. We have to reconnect the fixture wires to the wires coming out of the ceiling. We've got a black wire and a white wire and we want to twist together the wires of like color. We finish off by adding wire nuts to the connections.

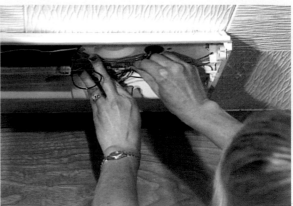

20 With the wires connected, Kim pushes the wires up out of the way, bending them to tuck tightly against the fixture.

21 With the wiring out of the way we're ready to install the frame. The frame slips into place around the fixture.

22 A couple of screws hold the frame in place.

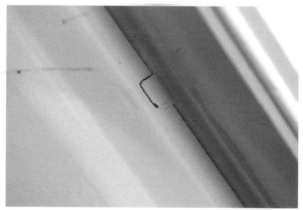

23 Now we can snap in the cover that conceals the wiring and ballast.

24 The ballast cover is held in place with a few tabs on the back side.

25 Fluorescent tubes, like the ones Kim is installing here, not only provide more light but consume less electricity and last longer than her old incandescent bulbs.

26 The last step is to install this diffuser that allows the fixture to cast a much softer light than bare fluorescent bulbs. With one fixture complete, we moved on to the second in the room.

27 The before and after shots of our handy work show what a difference good lighting can make.

Undercabinet Fluorescent Lighting

AN EASY FIX FOR THOSE SHADOWED COUNTERTOPS IN THE KITCHEN

One of the easiest task lights to install, fluorescent under-mount lights brighten up shaded areas inexpensively.

1 One of the darkest spots in your kitchen is a place where you most need light. And that's right here on the countertop underneath these wall cabinets.

2 The cabinets, and sometimes your body, create shadows making it difficult to see underneath. But there is a way to get light here without spending a lot of money or a lot of time.

3 The answer is a thin-profile fluorescent light designed specifically to go under cabinets. They are easy to install in just a few steps.

4 Remove the diffuser ...

5 ... and the bulb ...

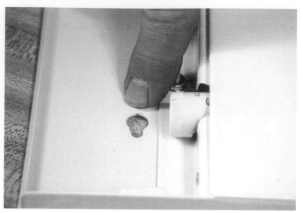

6 ... in order to reach the mounting hole.

7 Place the light fixture in the position you want it. Fixtures like this should go as far forward as possible.

8 Next, mark the position of the mounting holes. A piece of blue painter's tape on the cabinet makes it easier to see the mark.

9 Then drill a pilot hole ...

10 ... and attach the fixture using short, pan-head screws.

11 Fixtures like this usually have to be plugged in. The question is what do you do with all this cord? Well, by using plastic conduit like this, you can conceal it and end up with an installation that's very clean and professional looking.

12 Measure each section of conduit ...

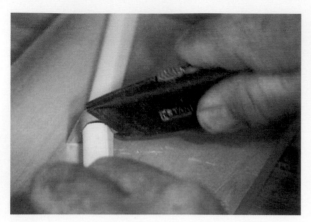

13 ... and cut it to length with a utility knife.

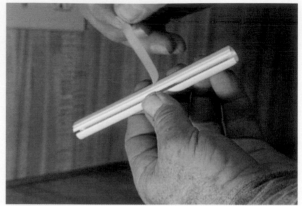

14 To install it, all you have to do is peel off the protective coating from the pressure sensitive back ...

15 ... and stick it in place.

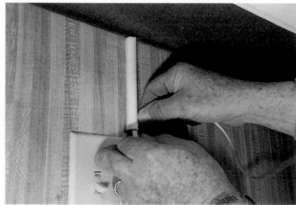

16 The electrical cord simply slips into the slot on the side.

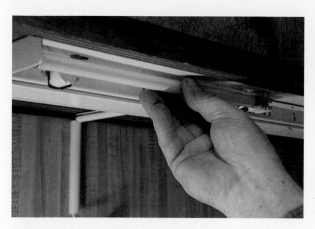

17 With the cord concealed, all that's left is to reinstall the bulbs ...

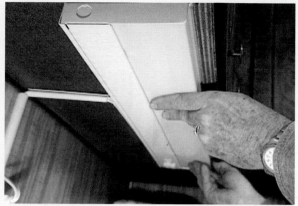

18 ... and the diffuser.

19 I can't think of an easier or less expensive way to get good work light into your kitchen. And best of all, it takes up practically no space.

Undercabinet LED Lighting

BRIGHTER, AND MORE ENERGY EFFICIENT TASK-LIGHTING FOR THE KITCHEN

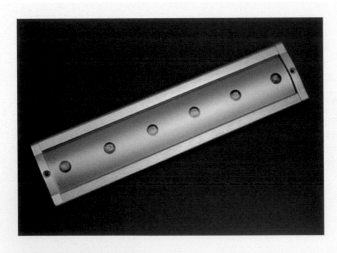

It stands to reason that if our kitchen is where we spend most of our waking hours, the lumens that brighten this space take on special importance. So today we address kitchen undercabinet lighting. This kind of illumination does double duty, providing both ambience and visibility.

1 It used to be that I never gave a lot of thought to lighting but I feel differently about that now, especially here in this room, the kitchen, because this is a social gathering spot and a workplace.

2 That means we need one kind of lighting for ambience and a different kind to work by. And there's been one spot in this kitchen where I've never really been happy with the light, and that's right up here underneath these cupboards.

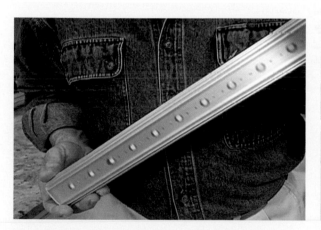

3 So I'm going to install some undercabinet lighting of a brand new type. It's an LED light and it has several advantages. For one, it's five times more energy efficient than an incandescent light and it has an incredibly long life — 60,000 hours.

4 Now to give you an idea of just how long that is, if you were to burn this 10 hours a day, 365 days a year, it would last more than 15 years. They're very attractive, low profile, in fact in my case, they're going to be virtually invisible.

5 And because they're low voltage, they're simple and safe to install. I've laid everything out to see where the lights will fit up underneath the cabinets. They are going to be powered by this transformer that will step the household current down to 12 volts AC.

6 I've decided I'm going to mount this transformer up here in the cabinet like this.

7 The power for the lighting is going to come from a switch that I'm going to put right in here. This is an old telephone junction box that I don't use anymore, so I'm going to take advantage of that location and install the switch there.

8 I've jumped ahead a bit and I've got my power run into the old phone junction box (see Adding A New Box, page 18). With the power in place, it's time to connect the lights.

9   What I need to do is run a wire from the cupboard down to the opening in the wall. I begin by using a bell hanger bit to drill through the cabinet back and into the wall cavity.

10   Next, I insert a flat metal wire called a fish tape into the hole ...

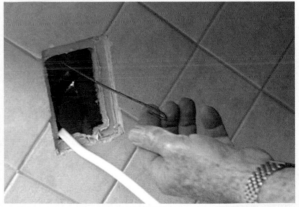

11   ... push it into the wall cavity ...

12   ... locate it with my other hand and pull it through the switch box opening.

13 I attach the cable to the loop in the end of the fish tape ...

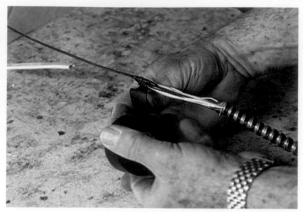

14 ... wrap it snugly with electrical tape ...

15 ... and pull the wire into the switch box opening through the wall ...

16 ... and into the cabinet above.

17 For this project I'm using armored cable. To cut through the outer metal jacket, I'm using a cable armor stripper.

18 Once cut, the armor is then pulled off, leaving the wires inside undamaged.

19 Now, I can slip the wires into an electrical box ...

20 ... and tighten the connector that clamps the armored outer cable in place.

21 The power cable (that I ran into the box earlier) is then pushed into the bottom of the box and held in place with a similar but slightly different connector.

22 To install the switch, I first strip a bit of insulation off the wire ends.

23 Then twist the white or neutral wires together ...

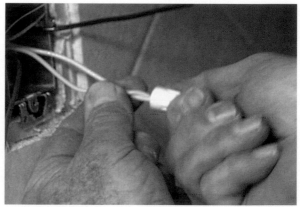

24 ... and secure them with a wire nut.

25 This switch has two black pigtails. One I connect to the black wire coming from the basement. The other I attach to the black wire going to the transformer.

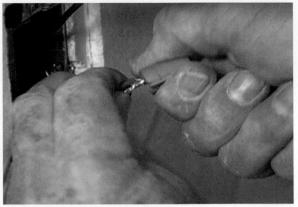

26 Finally, I connect the green ground wires together.

27 Now I set the switch into the box, secure it in place with mounting screws.

28 Then place the cover plate in position and install the screws.

29 Now we're ready to go to work on the lights. I'm going to start by removing this knockout from the transformer ...

30 ... and putting in a connector designed just for armored cable.

31 Now, I can slip the wires into place, tighten the set screw and set the transformer in position. Again, I connect the like colored wires to each other, green-to-green, black-to-black and white-to-white.

32 To run the low voltage wires to the first row of lights, I'm boring quarter inch holes through the cabinet shelves so I can feed the wire from the transformer to the underside of the cabinet.

33 These small plastic cable holders ...

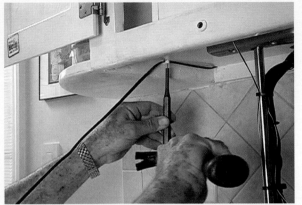

34 ... offer a simple and effective way to secure the wires while avoiding the risk of damaging the wires.

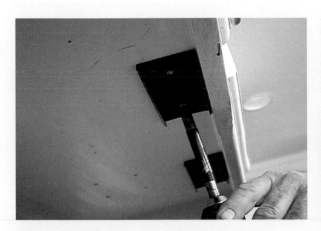

35 The light fixtures will be held in place with these brackets that are screwed to the underside of the cabinets.

36 Once everything's in place, the lights just snap into the brackets.

37 This is a modular lighting system. Low voltage wire plugs into the end of the fixture.

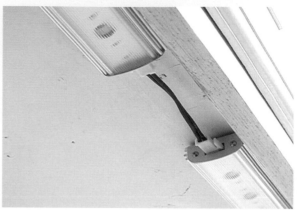

38 Short pigtails connect one unit to the next.

39 To run the wire to the adjacent cabinets, I've drilled a hole through the top of the first cabinet, and I'm going up ...

40 ... and across.

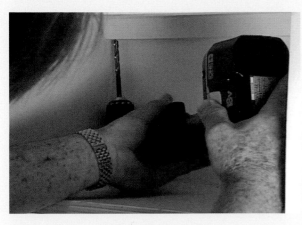

41 When I get to the other side of the window, I bore a small hole through the top of the cabinet, near the rear corner — and a hole through each shelf.

42 Then it's simply a matter of threading the wire from the top down ...

43 ... to the underside, once again.

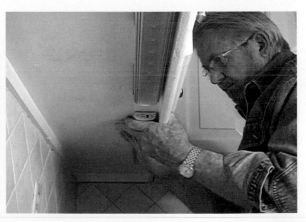

44 Then I put up more brackets, snap in the light fixtures ...

45 ... and plug in the wires.

46 To conceal the wire running across the moulding above the kitchen window, I'm using this plastic raceway. Peeling off the protective backing exposes a pressure sensitive adhesive on the bottom.

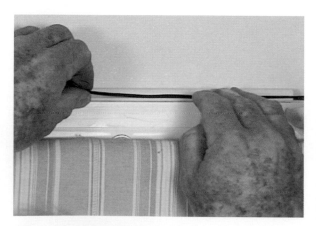

47 Once it's pressed in place, it will blend with its surroundings and completely conceal the wire that is pushed through a slot in the side.

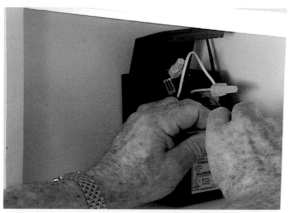

48 I have one small bit of wiring left to do. The low-voltage wires carrying power to the light fixtures need to be connected to the low-voltage output from the transformer. It's this reduction in current, from the potentially dangerous 120 volts to only 12 volts that makes this system safe and easy to work with.

49 You know, LED lighting is the wave of the future, but the good news is, you can have it in your own home right now. And I can't think of any better application for it than here in the kitchen.

Installing Track Lighting

TRACK LIGHTING LETS YOU PUT THE KIND OF LIGHT (DIRECT OR DIFFUSE) EXACTLY WHERE YOU WANT IT.

Sabrina Campbell is a hair stylist by profession, and she and her husband, Jim are interested in updating and improving the lighting in the salon. Track lighting is a perfect project for specific lighting needs.

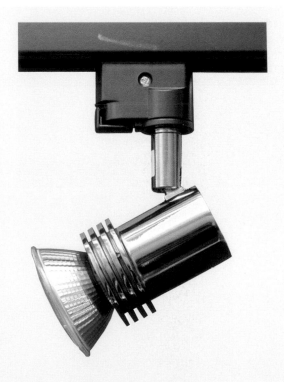

1   While fluorescent lighting is efficient, it's not always the most decorative or stylish. So we're going to replace these fixtures with Jim and Sabrina's help.

2   First we turn off the power to the overhead lights at the breaker panel.

3   As a precaution, we put tape over the switch.

4   Then we throw a few drop cloths over the cabinets and start removing the fluorescent fixtures. The plastic diffusers come off first.

5 Next the tubes are taken out ...

6 ... and then we remove the cover that is concealing the wiring.

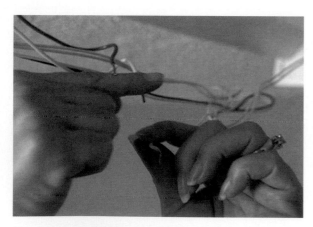

7 The wire connections are untwisted ...

8 ... and finally we remove the screws holding the fixtures to the ceiling.

9 ... and take the old fixture down.

10 A great advantage of track lighting is that it's flexible — you can put it exactly where you want it. Its disadvantage is that it's directional. It gives you spots of light, so I want to make sure that the light ends up where you need it.

11 Once we've identified just where Sabrina needs the most light, we decide to place blue masking tape on the ceiling to help us visualize where to best locate the track. In this case, a U-shaped pattern around the perimeter of the room looks like it will work best.

12 The power for this track is going to come from this wire right here. I've got a problem. There should be an electrical box right here and there isn't. So, I'm going to have to cut out a part of the ceiling and install one.

13 With a wallboard saw I make a few exploratory cuts and discover that the wires are right next to a ceiling joist. Using the box as a template, I first draw and then cut a hole in the wallboard, exposing the edge of the joist.

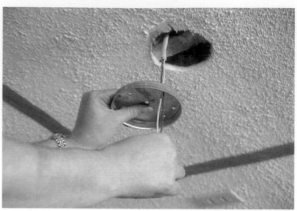

14 Sabrina then threads the wire through the back of the box and sets it in the hole we just cut in the ceiling.

15 Jim screws the box securely to the edge of the joist.

16 All that's required to convert any ceiling box into an electrical source for track lighting is this adapter, which is screwed on top of the junction box.

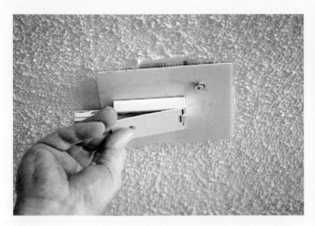

17 The wires coming from the ceiling are attached to terminals in the adapter and the cover is snapped into place.

18 Most track lighting should be installed between eighteen and twenty-four inches from the wall. So, we take down the masking tape, make our measurements, and snap a chalk line.

19 The track lighting system that we're about to put up is typical of most. It has three components; first, the track, which supports the light fixtures and conducts electricity.

20 Second, a variety of connectors that go into the end of each track section. Some make L-shaped turns, others T-shaped turns. There is also an adapter box that allows you to attach the track to an existing ceiling box.

101

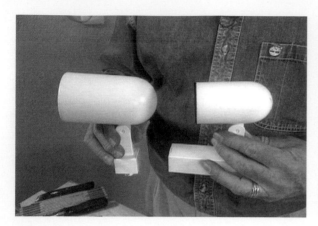

21 Finally, there are the light fixtures.

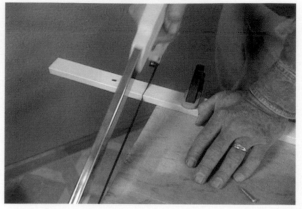

22 The track we're using today came in four and eight foot lengths, but this track can be cut to any length with a hacksaw.

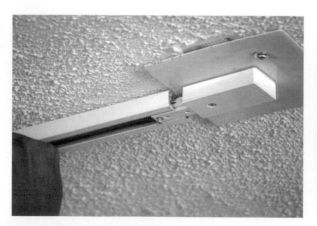

23 The first piece of track is plugged into the ceiling adapter ...

24 ... then we begin working our way around the room installing the longer sections.

25 The track is first aligned with the chalk line ...

26 ... and the mounting holes marked by drilling a small hole.

27 Then that hole is enlarged with a bigger drill bit, so that it will accommodate a toggle bolt.

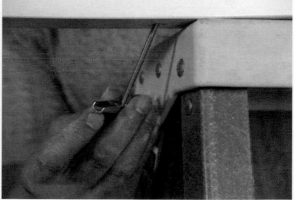

28 The toggle on a toggle bolt is a nut with folding wings.

29 As the bolt is pushed upward ...

30 ... the toggle springs open inside the ceiling ...

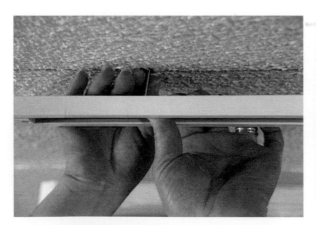

31 ... preventing the bolt from falling back out of the hole.

32 The thing I like most about track lighting is that it is a snap to install.

33 Sabrina, Jim and I work our way around the room connecting one section to the next.

34 Turning a corner is ad easy as plugging a corner adapter into a straight section.

35 Into the final sections we snap an end cap...

36 ... then tighten the toggle bolt, pulling the track snugly up against the ceiling.

37 Now were ready to install our fixtures.

38 Each fixture pushes up into the slot in the track at an angle ...

39 ... a turn of the base and the fixture contacts the power in the track and the light comes on.

40 A final twist locks the base into the track.

41 The great thing about track lighting is you can direct the light to illuminate almost anything you want.

42 Each lighting fixture has a job to do. Some will provide work light, some illumination for reading, while others will wash a wall or highlight an object.

43 With our lights placed, Sabrina has the perfect lighting to add atmosphere, and give her the working light she needs to do her job. Just a little bit off the side please.

Upgrade a Lamp to a Three-Way

MAKE YOUR SINGLE-WATTAGE LAMP DO THE WORK OF THREE, WITH THIS SIMPLE LIGHTING PROJECT

Three-way light bulbs have been around for a while, but that doesn't mean there are the same amount of three-way lamps. Don't replace the lamp to gain more variety, just do a simple upgrade.

1 The best lighting is the kind that you can adjust, make brighter or dimmer, not simply turn on or off. But the fact is you can make practically any lamp into a three-way lamp simply by changing the socket. It's simple. Let me show you how.

2 Start by unplugging the lamp ...

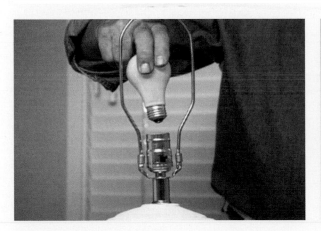

3 ... and unscrew the bulb.

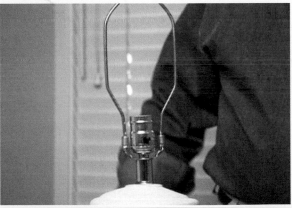

4 The wire bracket surrounding the bulb is known as a harp. There are two sleeves on either side of the harp where it meets the lamp. To remove the harp, first slide these sleeves up the harp ...

5 ... then squeeze the harp together to release it from the mounting bracket.

6 To remove the socket, look for the word *press* on the side of the socket.

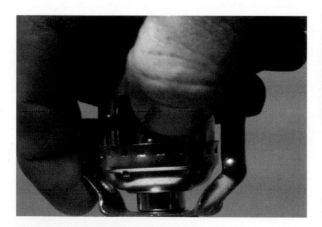

7 Push on that with your thumb ...

8 ... and pop it off.

9 Loosen the terminal screws ...

10 ... and remove the wires from the old socket.

11 Then attach the wires to the terminals on the new three-way socket.

12 Finally, replace the socket cover ...

13 ... reattach the harp ...

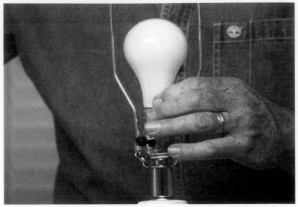

14 ... screw in the bulb ...

15 ... and replace the shade.

16 Plug the lamp back in ...

17 ... and now you've got lighting for just about any ...   ... mood ...

... or occasion.

Installing a Dimmer Switch

BORED WITH YOUR CEILING LIGHT?
HOW ABOUT ADDING SOME ATMOSPHERE?

Adding a simple or sophisticated dimmer to an existing light is a dramatic change for any room, but the project itself is a fifteen-minute project.

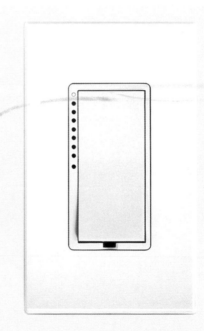

1 When it comes to indoor lighting, it's no longer a matter of black or bright, there's a whole range of shades in between, thanks to the wonderful world of dimmers.

2 When dimmer switches first came on the market, most looked like this.

3 Today, there's a lot more to choose from. You can have a slide dimmer with an on-off toggle at the bottom.

4 A mini slide with a push button on-off.

5 A mini slide with a decor-style rocker switch.

6 Or even smart dimmers that can store preset lighting themes and levels.

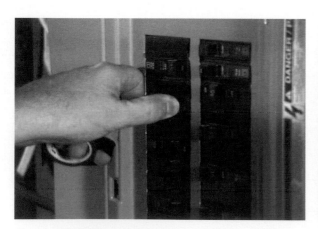

7 To replace a standard light switch with a dimmer, first turn off the power.

8 Then remove the cover plate ...

9 ... back out the two screws holding the switch ...

10 ... pull it out ...

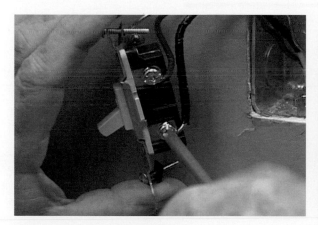

11 ... and disconnect the wires.

12 If the existing switch has wires wrapped around terminals like this, you'll need to either straighten the wire or snip off the hooked ends.

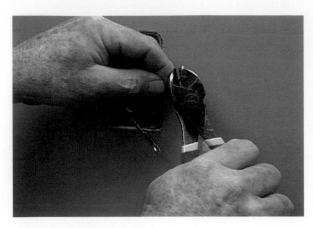

13 If you snip ...

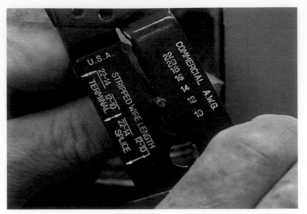

14 ... you'll probably need to strip off more insulation.

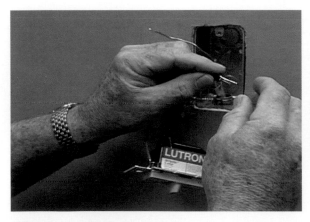

15 Dimmers typically come with pigtails that attach to the wires in the box.

16 To make the connections, twist the wires together and secure them with wire nuts, which are usually provided with the dimmer.

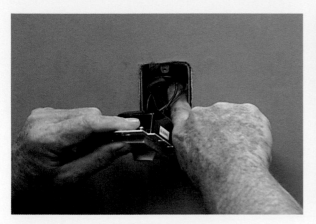

17 With the connections made, carefully fold the wires and push them to the back of the box.

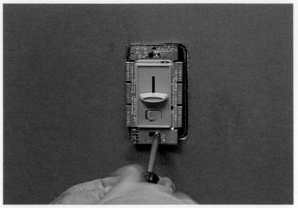

18 Set the dimmer switch in place and drive in the mounting screws.

19 Replace the switch plate, tighten the screws and you're done.

20 So, whether you want to set the mood or see to work, you'll find dimmers that are simple, smart and good looking.

Wireless Lighting Systems

TOO MANY LIGHT SWITCHES IN YOUR LIFE?
HOW ABOUT A CENTRAL WIRELESS CONTROLLER!

Whether it's your front porch light, the lamps in the living room, or the overhead lights in the game room, all can be controlled by centrally-located wireless controllers.

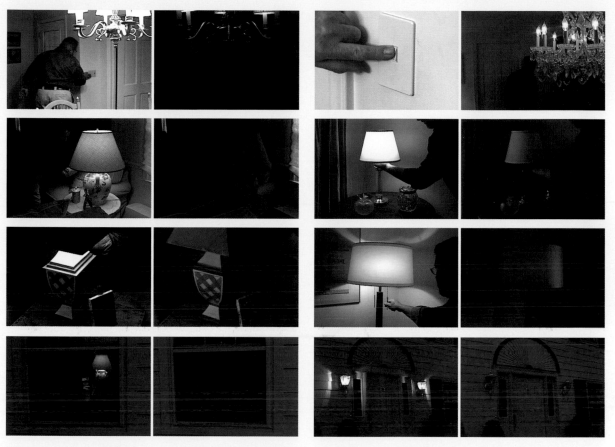

1 Every night before I turn in, I have a little bedtime ritual. I call this, the late-night-lights-out walkabout. Rather than hit twenty-five switches on my way to bed, I thought there should be an easier way. So I went on line and came across a product called Radio RA from Lutron Electronics.

2 The system is built around a master controller, special light switches and plug-in lamp modules.

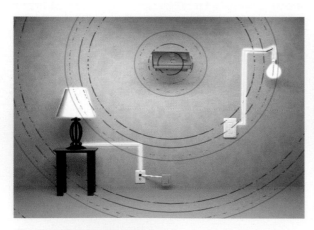 

3 The controller sends wireless radio signals that automatically turn lights and lamps on or off anywhere in the house. While I could have installed the system myself, I contacted a licensed electrician and Radio RA installer to get the best advice about our situation.

4 After asking questions about how we use lighting, we laid out a plan and several days later he returned with the materials for the system and went to work. He starts by removing the existing lighting switches and disconnecting the wires.

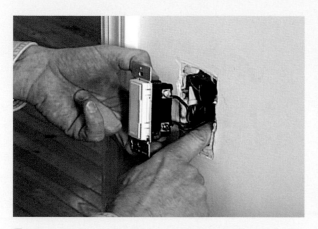

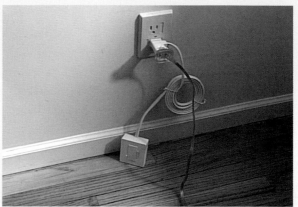

5 Each of the standard switches is replaced with an electronic dimmer, capable of receiving and sending the wireless radio signals.

6 Each wall receptacle into which a lamp is plugged, receives a lamp dimmer.

7 These install easily, requiring no wiring and can be used to control virtually any lighting device that plugs into a wall receptacle. Each one can be set to turn the lamp up to any desired level of brightness.

8 The master bedroom will get a controller that plugs into an outlet and sits on the bedside table.

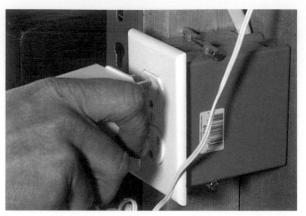

9 In the basement, a timer is installed, requiring only a few screws ...

10 ... and an available outlet.

11 Among other things, the timer can turn the outside lights on at dusk and off at midnight using wireless radio waves.

12 Its built in microprocessor adjusts the turn-on time each day and automatically compensates for daylight-savings time.

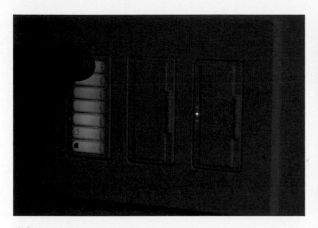

13 The next time I arrive home at night, the controller that's installed at the door ...

14 ... will let me turn on all the lights in and out of the house with a single push of a button.

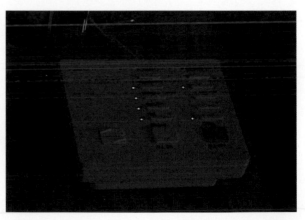

15 And now if I want to go from reading in the family room to watching TV ...

16 ... I can change the lighting scene without ever leaving my seat.

Automatic Light Controllers

BY SCREWING IN AN ADAPTER YOU CAN ADD A DIMMER, TIMER AND MORE TO YOUR TABLE LAMP.

With the turn of a screw, (actually a screwed-in accessory) you can change the lighting in and out of your house, and allow programmable and touch-sensitve control.

1 Welcome to the wonderful world of light controllers. Simple screw-in devices that can convert any floodlight, lamp or exterior fixture into one that turns on or off automatically.

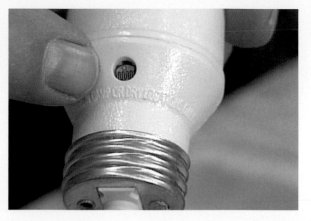

2 This controller has a built-in photoelectric cell.

3 The device installs in any lamp or fixture ...

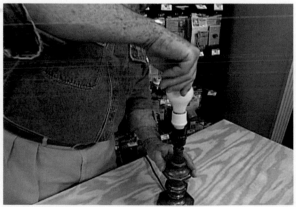

4 ... then the bulb screws into it.

5 By shading the sensor with my hand to simulate darkness ...

6 ... the controller senses this and turns on the lamp.

7 This version converts just about any lamp into a touch-control lighting device. The device screws into the standard socket and the bulb is screwed into the device.

8 Once it's in place, I can touch any part on the metal base and switch the lamp on or off — even three-way bulbs will work with this device.

9 A lighting control like this incorporates a timer ...

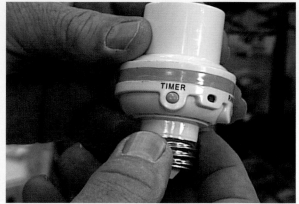

10 ... that will turn a lighting fixture on and off based on how your program it.

11 It allows you to have light precisely when you want it, indoors or outdoors.

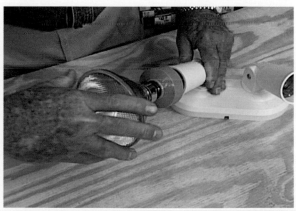

12 By simply screwing in this photoelectric controller, any exterior floodlight can be converted to one that turns on automatically as darkness falls. Bottom line, indoors or out, if your light fixture has a bulb, then you can make it automatic.

129

Outdoor

Low-Voltage Outdoor Lighting

TURN YOUR NIGHTTIME YARD INTO A VIEW TO BEHOLD

I spend a day at a stately Dallas neighborhood to help brighten one homeowner's life by installing a low voltage outdoor lighting system.

1 We're at Cynthia Hirsch's house, and she wants to showcase her beautiful home by day and by night. So, we'll put in an easy-to-install outdoor lighting system that will make her house glow and sparkle after dark.

2 One of the yard features she'd like to showcase is this impressive pecan tree. It's the largest tree in the front yard, so she would like to try and highlight it as much as possible.

3 At the entrance to the driveway Cynthia points out another lighting need. Visitors seem to have difficulties staying on the drive, and have damaged some of her sprinkler heads. She wants to add some lights to define the driveway and the pathway into the house.

4 We first sketch out a plan, determining the location and particular lighting requirement needed for each section of the yard.

5 I suggest we use several ground-level well lights ...

6 ... to cast a soft glow on the front of the house.

7 We'll also use one of these fixtures for the pecan tree as well.

8 To accentuate a pair of smaller trees in the front yard we'll use vertical beam lights. They are similar to the well lights but cast a more directional beam.

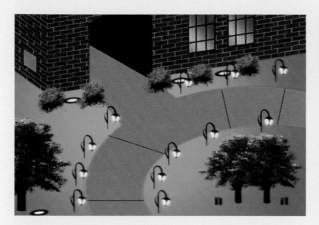

9 Finally, we'll line the driveway with decorative lanterns. Low-voltage lighting systems require a power converter that makes low voltage lighting safe. The controller box reduces the household current of 110 volts down to 12 volts.

10 We want to mount the controller on the wall here. It needs to be at least 12 inches above the ground. To locate the mounting bracket, we start by making a couple of starter holes with a spring-loaded center punch.

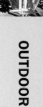

11 I then use a carbide-tipped masonry bit to bore holes in the mortar joint, where it's easier to drill.

12 After inserting lead anchors we attach the mounting bracket with screws.

13 The controller box then slides onto the mounting bracket.

14 Next we attach the low-voltage electrical cable to the terminals on the power supply.

15 One cable will carry power to the lanterns along the driveway and will light the pecan tree. The cable will then cross the driveway and power the vertical beams under the small trees as well as additional lanterns on the other side of the driveway.

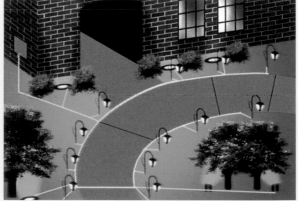

16 A second cable will carry low voltage current to the well lights (flooding the front of the house) and nearby lanterns.

17 We want to run some wire along the edge of the driveway right here. Using a garden spade we pry up the sod ...

18 ... just enough to tuck the wire neatly out of sight.

19 Then we gently push the grass back into place.

20 To up-light this tree we're going to use this well light. It gets buried at ground level, which is a big advantage when you're mowing your lawn because you don't have to take it out.

21 A couple of things to keep in mind as far as placement goes. The light needs to be about three or four feet from the trunk. Also, you want to look up and pick a spot on the tree that will allow the light to go as far up into the tree as possible.

22 I'm thinking that maybe the best location is about right here.

23 We use a clamshell post hole digger to dig holes for the light fixture.

24 Next, we use the spade to cut a wedge-shaped groove in the sod, then insert a short length of cable and press the sod back into place.

25 Then we place the light into the ground ...

26 ... and connect it to the power cable.

27 This light system uses a connector with sharp prongs that bite through the insulation ...

28 ... making contact with the wire inside as the top ring is screwed down.

29 Once the cables are connected together we fill in the space around the light with sand.

30 This is the fixture Cynthia picked out for the driveway. There are a couple of rules about spacing on these. They need to be ten feet apart and should be set back from the edge of the driveway about fourteen inches so cars don't hit them.

31 These couldn't be simpler to install. Just push the stake into the ground like this.

32 We use our spade to run the wire out to the edge of the driveway where our power line is already run.

33 Now we have a small problem. We've got to cross the driveway here. So, to do that we're going to take advantage of this expansion joint.

34 This joint is to keep the concrete from cracking. As we pry this wooden strip from the joint, we're left with an ideal trench for running a cable across the driveway. We lay the cable in the bottom of the joint and put in a new piece of expansion material.

35 We check to be sure the new expansion piece is flush to the driveway, then fill any gaps on the sides of the strips with sand and use a broom to work it into the crevices, sweeping away the excess.

36 Now we can light the smaller trees on the opposite side. This is a 20-watt halogen vertical-beam light. It's going to light up this small tree right here.

37 We'll place this light about six inches from the trunk since we'll want to cast a lot of illumination on the trunk itself.

38 Next we move on to the front of the house. To flood the front walls of the house with light we're going to use 50-watt halogen, well lights. These have a sealed beam, so, even though water may collect on the surface it won't damage the fixture.

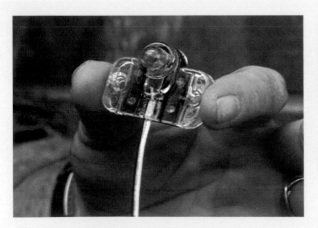

39 We're also installing a light sensor that will automatically turn the system on and off.

40 You can mount this anywhere, but the important thing is to avoid mounting this in heavily shadowed areas, or areas where you have artificial lighting at night.

41 We can choose a dusk-to-dawn schedule or set it to remain on for a specified number of hours after dusk.

42 To complete the installation, we'll pop on the cover ...

43 ... and plug the unit in.

44 The new lights are low voltage, but they have a megawatt impact that makes the home glow and sparkle.

Exterior Lamp and Post

MORE THAN JUST LIGHT, A LAMP POST SAYS, "WELCOME".

I don't know about you but I'm a big fan of curb appeal. I want my house to look nice from the street and to be welcoming when friends come over. So I decided to put a lamp post in the front yard.

1 Here in the northeast, it gets pretty cold. And the ground can freeze down two feet or more and create what's called a frost-heave effect. If the ground freezes beneath the end of the light post, it can actually push it up out of the ground.

2 To avoid that, I'll make the hole at least two and a half feet deep. I could use a post hole digger but I'm going to do it the easy way — with a post-hole auger that can be rented at almost any home improvement or rental center.

3 The trick here is to hang on tight. There are plenty of rocks in this soil and I'm bound to hit a few.

4 I got my thirty-two inches. The frost shouldn't get under this post.

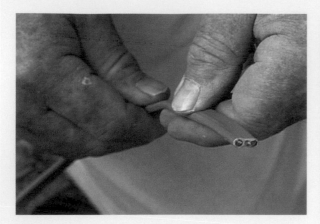

5 I've had an electrician run power to the post using a special outdoor- or underground-rated cable. The wires are encased in PVC. The wire has to be buried at least twelve inches underground.

6 A couple of inches of crushed rock In the bottom of my post hole will help drain away any water that might collect there.

7 The post I've chosen is pre-stained and made of solid cedar. Cedar is lightweight, yet strong — a rare combination. It's also highly resistant to rock, decay and insects because of the natural oils produced by the cedar tree.

8 The post has been pre-bored for the wire which is going to enter below grade — or below ground — and then run up the center and come out the top. The manufacturer has been kind enough to put this piece of string in here.

146

9 So all I have to do is loop the wire through the string and pull it from this point right up through the end. I secure the loop by wrapping it with electrical tape.

10 Then I push the wire into the hole ...

11 ... go to the opposite end and pull it through using the string.

12 My wire is in the post and coming out the top. Now I'm ready to set the post in the hole.

13 This strap-on post level will leave my hands free.

14 To hold the post in position, I drive in a couple of stakes into the yard, then clamp a strip of wood between the stakes and post.

15 I loosen the clamps and adjust as needed. Once the post is perfectly vertical, I re-tighten the clamps and the post stays just where I want it. Although this solid cedar post is highly rot-resistant, it's not rot proof. The maker suggests that I not set it in concrete.

16 Concrete forms a collar around the post, and If the post shrinks, water can get in the gap, get trapped there and cause the post to rot prematurely. So this one is going in plain old dirt. After adding a few inches of soil, I compact it using a 2x4. With the hole backfilled and compacted I can remove the clamps and braces.

17 This cedar sleeve will turn an otherwise ordinary post into something special.

18 It slips over the top and is held in place with finish nails.

19 To keep water out, I apply caulk to the joint and smooth out the bead using my finger.

20 This post cap also adds a classic touch and incorporates a mounting base with the light fixture.

21 I'm working alone today, so I've made this clamp-on shelf.

22 The plan is to lay the light fixture on it while I connect the wires.

23 The electrical connections are pretty basic. Split the PVC covering ...

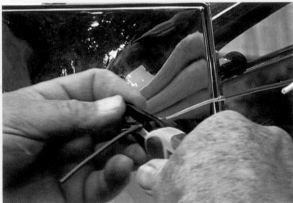

24 ... strip off the wire insulation ...

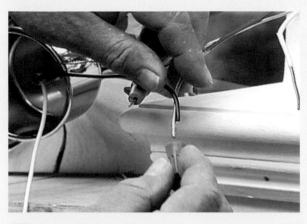

25 ... secure the wires together using wire nuts ...

26 ... and wrap the whole thing tightly with electrical tape for some added weather proofing.

27 Now I can slip the lantern over the mounting base, install a screw ...

28 ... check for level and install the remaining fasteners.

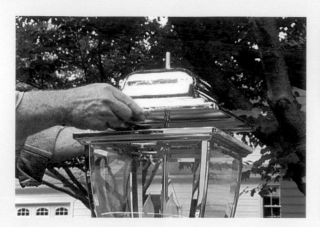

29 All that's left is to set the lantern top in place ...

30 ... then add the trim ring ...

31 ... and screw on the finial.

32 You know, there's something very welcoming about a lamp post.

33 I guess it says yes, we're home, come on in.

34 For our friends and family we can now say, we'll leave the light on for you.

Landscape Lighting

**OUTDOOR LIGHTING IS FOR THE WHOLE YARD,
NOT JUST THE TREES.**

I think of my back yard as an extension of my home. So, today we are going to do some exterior decorating in the form of low-voltage landscape lighting. This is a terrific do-it-yourself project if you have a good plan, use the right devices and know a few simple installation tricks.

1 I've asked lighting designers, Gary Novosel and Rachel Pfeiffer to help me out. Gary says he likes to start with the theme of the yard, find out what's useful and start with that.

2 My theme is very much about trees, so that's where we'll begin.

3 Gary explains that one way to light trees is from the ground upward; a technique called uplighting. My Japanese maple is a good candidate.

4 These trees are uniquely sculptural and the branch structure is open and beautiful with twists and turns.

155

5 Trees can also be lit from the top downward, to simulate moonlight filtering through the branches. The sunlight playing on the patio gives an indication of what's possible.

6 One of my favorite daytime landscaping elements is my pond. I ask Gary if that offers an opportunity for lighting at night.

7 He sees the focal point as the waterfall, so we'll plan on getting a bit of light on that.

8 He also wants us to see the whole pond with the plantings. He points out that the tree next to the pond gives another opportunity for "moonlighting" and up-lighting.

9 Gary proposes installing fixtures on both the left and right sides of the arbor, down at grade level, which will illuminate the entire structure.

10 On this arbor, Rachel suggests using a light at the top, rather than accenting it from the bottom.

11 For this small fountain, Rachel suggests putting a fixture in the water to get some sparkle and reflection.

12 For this stately Beech tree, Gary suggests more uplighting. Illuminating the entire area will have the effect of bringing the tree into the room at night.

13 Rachel and Gary make a rough sketch of the property. Not terribly elaborate — just enough to show position and relationship of the key features.

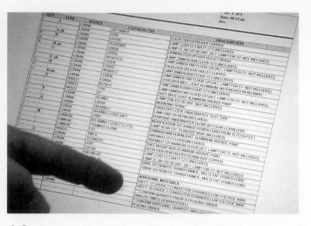

14 Back at their workshop, they create lighting specifications that will indicate what fixtures, bits-and-pieces and parts will be required so I know exactly what to order.

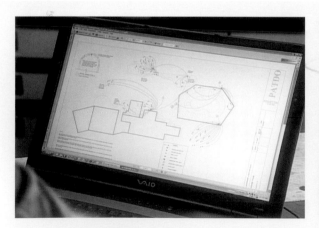

15 Here's the finished plan that Gary and Rachel have worked up, showing the location of every light.

16 Once I approve it all, they mark the fixture locations with landscaping flags.

17 A few day later, I have all my materials and I'm ready to go to work. These transformers are what put the *low* in low voltage. They'll reduce my household current of 120 volts down to about 12 volts, which is relatively safe to work with.

18 From the outside, they look like metal boxes, but inside, it's a different story.

19 In this transformer from Loran, there are a series of terminals to which the light fixture wires will be connected.

20 These fuses protect four separate circuits.

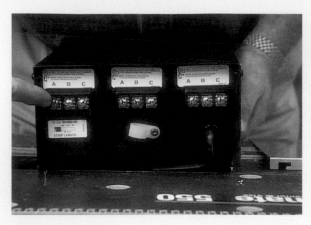

21 This transformer from Intermatic has the wire terminals on the bottom.

22 I use stainless-steel screws to mount the transformers to the side of the house. Dipping them in silicone caulk helps prevent any water leaks.

23 The mounting bracket on the back has slotted holes that slip over the screw heads.

24 This plastic conduit will protect the low-voltage wires from any damage where they're above ground.

25 Once the conduit's in place, I slip the wires inside, pull them into the box ...

26 ... strip off the insulation, twist the strands ...

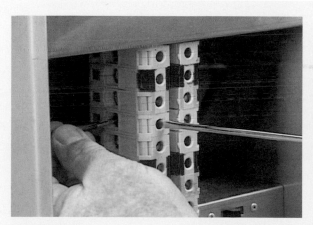

27 ... and attach the ends to the terminals.

28 Transformers can be turned on and off manually or automatically. In this Loran unit, I'm installing a photoelectric cell and a timer. The photoelectric device will turn the lights on at dusk ...

29 ... and a timer will shut them off at whatever time I choose.

30 Once everything's in place, I back fill around the plastic conduit ...

31 ... put the cover on the transformer and plug into a nearby outlet.

32 Since the terminals on this Intermatic transformer are on the bottom, I'm going to make the connections first ...

33 ... then mount the transformer.

34 This model comes with a built-in timer.

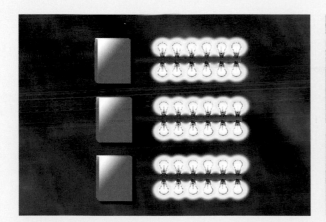

35 Here's where I need to check the lighting plan. Depending on its size, a single transformer can only provide power to so many fixtures. It's important to balance the load and use enough transformers to handle the demand.

36 This uplight fixture from Loran needs to be spliced into the low-voltage wire.

163

37 I cut the wire near each fixture location ...

38 ... strip off the insulation ...

39 ... twist the fixture wire and line wire together ...

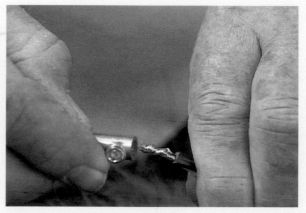

40 ... slip the wires into this brass barrel ...

41 ... tighten the set screw ...

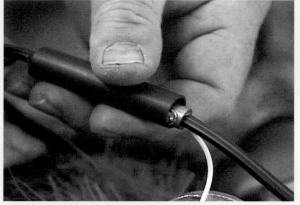

42 ... slip a piece of tubing over the joint ...

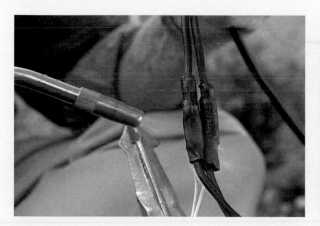

43 ... then heat it with a propane torch. This special tubing shrinks as it's heated and silicone inside melts, providing a permanent watertight seal.

44 I'm driving a straight pry bar into the ground to create a hole for the mounting stake.

45 After setting it in place, I use the end of the mallet handle to compact the soil around the stake.

46 Here in these flower beds, I'll dig a shallow trench ...

47 ... fold the wire back upon itself ...

48 ... and cover it up. The extra wire I've left will allow me to relocate the fixture later if I want to.

49 This light fixture from Intermatic has a different type of wire connector.

50 These two interlocking clips can be attached anywhere along the line wire.

51 Two prongs penetrate the insulation and make contact with the wire conductor inside. In this case, it's not necessary to cut the wire to make a connection.

52 As with the other uplight fixtures, this model includes a spike that sinks into the ground to secure the light.

53 The best way to run wire along the edge of a driveway to a patio is by cutting a narrow slot, using a flat garden spade, leveraging the spade against the pavement.

54 A thin piece of wood makes a handy tool for pushing the wire to the bottom of the groove.

55 The slot can be easily closed by pressing it down by foot.

56 The same technique is used to lay wire across a lawn. I'm working the garden spade back and forth to create a narrow "V" in the ground, about six inches deep and, again, pushing the wire to the bottom.

57 As I enter the bed, I slip a foot-long piece of plastic conduit over the wire to protect it from damage I might inflict when I'm doing my edging next spring. To close the groove,

58 The uplights that we've put in so far, so-called bullet lights, are designed to sit on top of the ground. That's fine in bushes and shrubs, but out in the grass I'm going to be mowing and having something like this sticking up — well, that could be a problem.

59 So, I'm going to use well lights that are designed to be put into the ground so that the top is flush with the surface. Using a post spade, I first remove the sod ...

60 ... then switch to a post hole digger.

61 In the bottom of the hole, I like to place a little gravel for drainage.

62 When the hole is the correct depth ...

63 ... I make the wire connections. This fixture from Loran calls for a watertight splice.

64 Once I'm finished, I lay the wire in the trench, backfill the hole and close it up.

65 Intermatic's version of the well light is slightly larger in diameter and a bit shallower.

66 This one, like most Intermatic low-voltage fixtures, uses the pressed-together insulation-piercing connector.

67 Now I want to do some downlighting, which involves putting a fixture up in the tree and casting the light downward. I'm using this compact fixture, and all I have to do is screw the lens on and then take it up about twenty feet up. Now, who says I don't do my own stunts?

68 The trick, as it turns out, is to hang onto the light and clutch the tree limb at the same time while I attach, then aim the fixture.

69 The pond will be lit from above and below. This Loran underwater fixture — called the Porpoise — is omnidirectional and comes with a weighted base.

70 Intermatic's underwater light uses a spot or flood lamp and has a ring base that can be weighted.

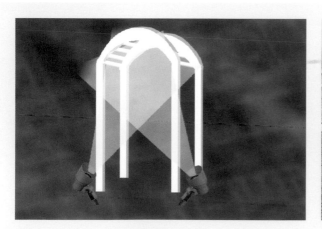

71 The arbor will be illuminated by four uplights, placed in the ground at each corner. I'll get more lighting if the light beams are crisscrossed, rather than being aimed straight up.

72 These slim, solid-copper fixtures from Loran will tuck out of the way and darken naturally when exposed to weather.

73 Another option here would be to use these copper fixtures from Intermatic.

74 The other arbor will be lit from the top downward with this perforated fixture that will glow at night.

75 And my fountain? Well, it gets a small underwater light, no larger than a test tube.

76 Obviously the effects of landscape lighting can only be appreciated at night.

77 That's why I set the lights temporarily in place. Then go out after dark and tweak them to get just the effect I'm looking for.

78 From design, to plan, to installation, to finished product.

79 Now it's time to sit back ...

80 ... and take in the show.

81 What I love so much during the day ...

82 ... has taken on a whole new look at night.

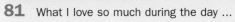

SECTION FOUR

...And More

Installing a Programmable Thermostat

SAVE MONEY AND ENERGY WITH A SIMPLE UPGRADE

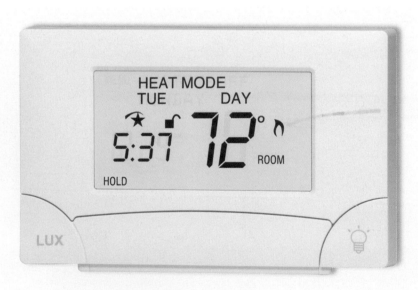

By programming your thermostat to keep your home cooler (in the winter) or warmer (in the summer) when you're not home, you can save energy and money. Just set it and forget it!

1 Installing a programmable thermostat can cut your energy costs by up to thirty-three percent. It's easy to do with a few simple steps.

2 First remove the decorative cover or trim piece from the existing thermostat.

3 Underneath you'll find mounting screws.

4 Remove these and the thermostat mechanism.

5 Most thermostats have four or five wires connected to terminals ...

6 ... that are labeled by letter.

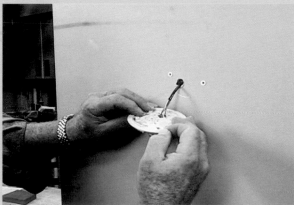

7 Next remove the mounting screws from the base ...

8 ... and pull it away from the wall.

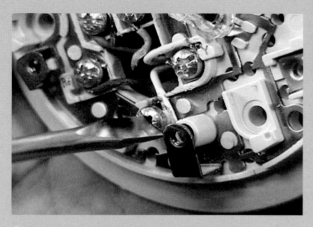

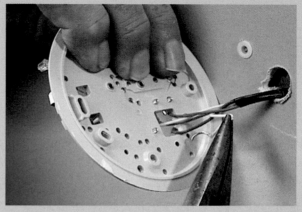

9 One by one, disconnect the wires from the terminals.

10 Pull each one out and label it as you go.

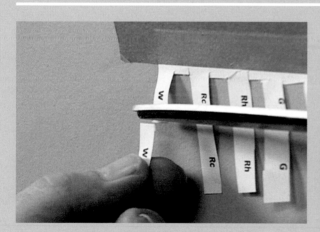

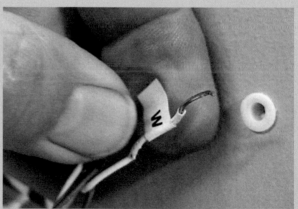

11 I made these labels with a computer printer and sprayed the back with contact cement.

12 You may not have to do this as many of the thermostats include labels in the package.

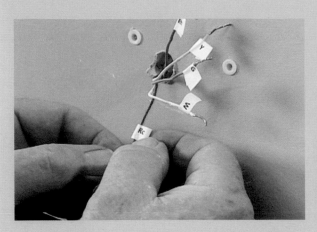

13 What's important here is to make sure the labels match the lettering on the terminals. They have nothing to do with the wire colors.

14 Place the new base in position on the wall ...

15 ... and mark the location of the mounting holes.

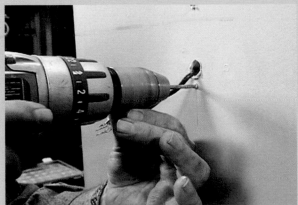

16 Drill the holes ...

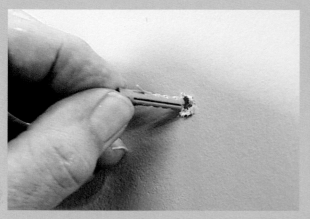

17 ... insert plastic anchors, tapping them into place with a hammer ...

18 ... and mount the base plate.

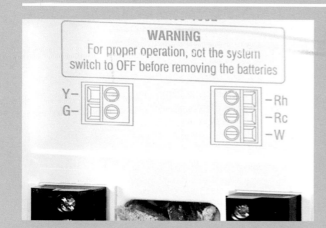

19 This thermostat has a printed wiring diagram. Remember those labels?

20 All you have to do is attach the labelled wires to the corresponding terminals. No guesswork, no trial and error.

21 Finally, snap on the cover and you're finished.

22 For a sleeker look, consider this flush-mounted thermostat.

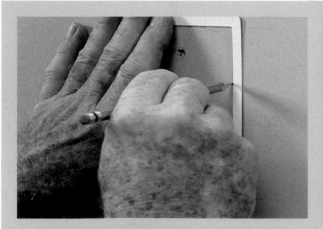

23 To install it, trace the inside of this template that's included with the thermostat.

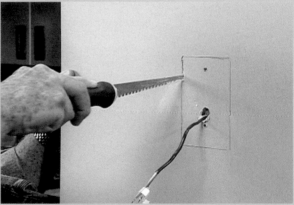

24 Cut out the marked opening using a wallboard saw and set the recessed housing in place.

25 As you begin tightening the screws on the front of the housing, wings flip out on the backside of the wall.

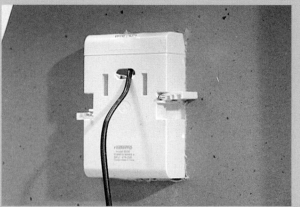

26 Continued tightening pulls the wings snuggly against the surface, holding the box securely in place.

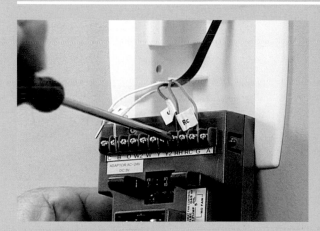

27 Then connect the labeled wires to the corresponding terminals.

28 And finally, slip the thermostat into the housing and snap it in place.

Replacing a Doorbell

NOT WORKING? OR JUST NEED A NEW TUNE? A DOORBELL IS EASY TO REPLACE IN JUST A FEW MINUTES.

Door chimes have come a long way. You can play your school's fight song or change tunes to match the holiday. Upgrading your doorbell is a simple home project.

1 A lot of people tell me that sometimes they just find their doorbells boring. Other times, downright annoying. But the point is, you don't have to live with a doorbell you don't like. It's easy enough to change it. Come on inside and I'll show you how.

2 Keep in mind that while it's operated by low voltage, it still is an electrically operated device, so you want to turn off the power at the circuit breaker.

3 Many doorbell covers, like this one, simply pop off. Some require you to take out a couple of screws.

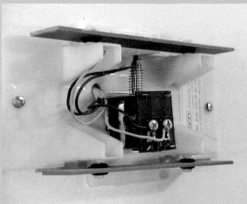

4 The next step is to take off the wires which are attached to these terminals. But notice that the terminals are marked.

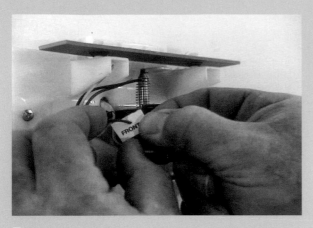

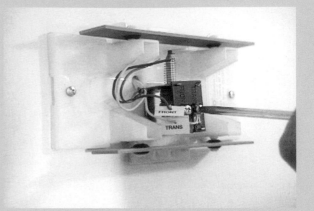

5 One reads "front" and the other reads "tran" or transformer. So, we want to mark those wires before we disconnect them. We're going to use these little tags that came with our new doorbell.

6 Now, with those in place we can go ahead and begin to loosen these terminal wires, then remove the screws that are holding the doorbell to the wall.

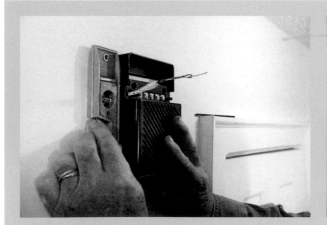

7 To install the new doorbell, we'll slip the wires through this hole in the back and check to make sure that it's vertical or plumb on the wall.

8 Then mark the location for the new screw holes ...

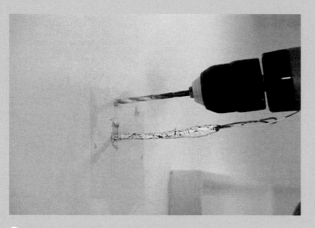

9 ... drill the mounting holes and insert the plastic anchors ...

10 ... then attach the doorbell with screws.

11 All that's left is to reconnect the wires to the terminals, matching the labels to the terminal designations, ...

12 ... and snap the cover in place. And there you go. You can choose from doorbells that will play as many as sixty different tunes!

189

Installing a Ceiling Fan

IMPROVE HEATING AND AIR CONDITIONING EFFICIENCY WITH THIS SIMPLE AFTERNOON PROJECT

Diane Drake loves to relax on her back porch, enjoying the sights and sounds of nature. Often it's just too doggone hot for comfort. So, she's asked me to help install a ceiling fan

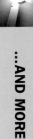

1 Diane takes me out to her back porch and shows me the location where she'd like to add her ceiling fan.

2 An older-style porch light is mounted on the ceiling and will make a fine location for the new fan.

3 For safety, we've shut the power off at the breaker box, and, we're using fiberglass ladders (wood is also fine). Even with the power off, it's a good practice to be extra safe. Using a screwdriver with an insulated handle we start taking down the fixture by removing the screws.

4 With the screws removed, the glass shade pulls away easily.

5 The bulb is next, then the mounting screws for the socket.

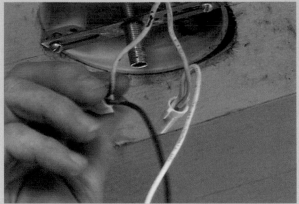

6 With the insulation removed, the wires are exposed. The wire nuts can be removed and the wires disconnected.

7 It's at this point that a lot of people make a mistake. They try to attach the fan to the existing electrical box that was designed only to support the weight of a light.

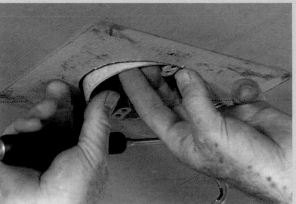

8 We're going to take this out and replace it with a heavy-duty box.

9 The new box slips inside the ceiling cavity and braces between the studs using these points, but let me show you how it works on this mock-up.

10 The brace simply slips through the hole in the ceiling ...

11 ... move it around until it's over the hole and then, rotate this bar ...

12 ... until those sharp points bite into the sides of the joist. This is what enables the brace to support the weight of the fan.

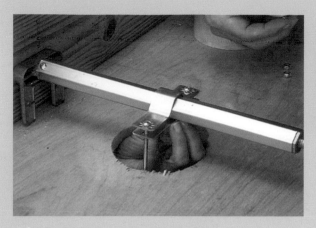

13 Next attach the mounting bracket to the brace, attach the nuts that hold the bracket in place ...

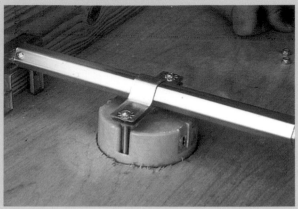

14 ... and slide the electrical box into position and fasten it in place with nuts. It's easy here in our mock-up, but working blind inside the ceiling is a little more of a challenge.

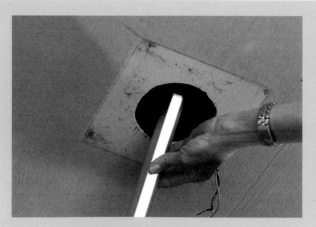

15 I slide the mounting brace into the hole in the ceiling and repeat the steps we just showed using our mock-up.

16 The box is in place and the nuts can be attached to secure our box adequately to support the weight of the ceiling fan.

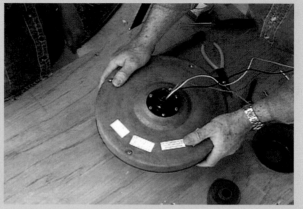

17 The final step is to attach a mounting bracket to the junction box. The ceiling fan will hang from this.

18 Now we turn our attention to the fan. This is the fan motor and we're going to have to do a little assembly before we can attach it to the mounting bracket.

19 We're going to install the fan twelve inches down from the ceiling for better air circulation. First we'll run the wires through the extension rod, attach the rod to the motor with this holding pin ...

20 ... then secure the holding pin with this cotter pin.

21 Because this fan is going to be outdoors, we don't want moisture leaking into the motor. We slip this rubber boot over the extension rod and slide it all the way down.

22 Next we slide this decorative canopy over the extension rod. It's one of the last pieces to put in place, but we need it on before going any further.

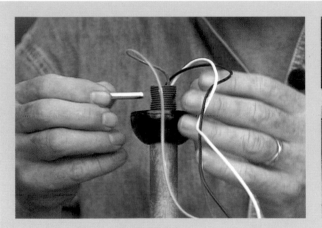

23 This plastic ball goes on the end of the rod. It's going to allow us to attach the fan to the bracket we mounted on the ceiling. We secure it in place with another holding rod and cotter pin.

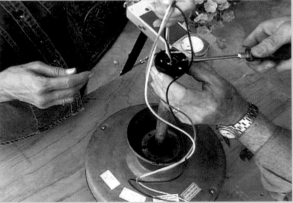

24 To hold that in position there is a set screw right here.

25 To hang the fan, the ball slips into the bracket we put up earlier. We then wire the fan, hooking all wires of the same color together and adding wire nuts and some electrical tape to secure everything.

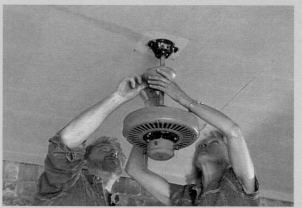

26 Now that all the wires have been connected we're going to tuck them back up in the box neatly like that and then slide the canopy up and screw it in place.

27 The fan blades screw onto the blade brackets. I generally leave the first screw a little lose to leave a little leeway to get the second screw in place, then tighten all the screws.

28 Well, the sun is going down and it's cooled off a bit, but I've got to tell you the breeze from this fan feels terrific.

Installing a Dishwasher

MORE THAN JUST AN ELECTRICAL PROJECT, IT'S ONE THAT YOU CAN TACKLE ON YOUR OWN AND SAVE MONEY

Sandi Fix just moved into her first home and one of the first upgrades she wanted to tackle was replacing the outdated dishwasher that was noisy and rattled. I told her I'd give her a hand.

1 Like many first-time homeowners, Sandi Fix knows her new house needs a lot of work. One of the first things she wants to tackle is replacing the aging dishwasher. It's noisy and just doesn't work the way it should.

2 We start by turning off the power at the breaker box.

3 Then, tape down the switch so no one will come along and accidentally turn it on a again.

4 We remove the access panel at the bottom of the appliance where all the plumbing and electrical connections are located. The panel may be attached with screws or bolts or simply snapped in place.

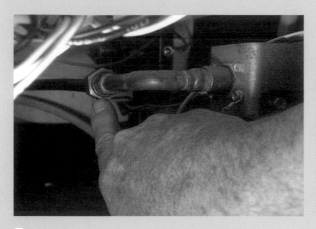

5 Here's the water line coming in right here.

6 The electrical connects here.

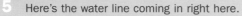

7 This large hose is the drain.

8 Our next job is to remove the cover to access the electrical lines.

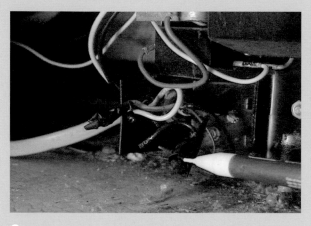

9 We test the wires to make sure that they're not live before we go ahead and cut them.

10 No noise from our tester, so we're safe to cut the wires. Next, we turn off the water supply to the dishwasher.

11 Then we slip a pan under the water connection as there may be a little bit of water leaking out when we loosen the connection. Then Sandi loosens up the connection on the water line using one of my favorite tools ...

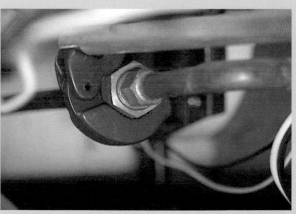

12 ... the basin wrench. It's designed just for getting into tight spaces like this.

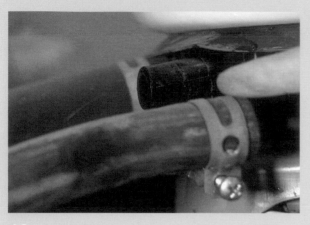

13 Next she disconnects the drain line. First she releases the clamp, then with a little tug pulls the hose free.

14 Now that all of our major connections are separated, we can remove the screws from the bracket holding the dishwasher to the cabinet.

15 We each take a side of the old dishwasher, wiggle it a little, and pull it out from the cabinet space. As appliances go, dishwashers aren't all that heavy, but they can be awkward.

16 It's also smart to pull the old appliance out slowly to make sure it doesn't catch on anything that could be pulled loose.

17 With the dishwasher out of the way, we can see a hole in the back wall. While we can't be sure if it's a man-made or rodent-made hole, it's a good idea to patch it while we've got the dishwasher out.

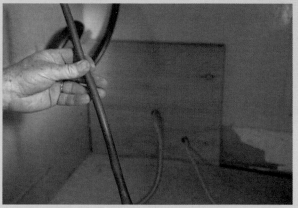

18 Along with patching the hole, I replace the old copper water lines ...

19 ... with new flexible versions.

20 We're ready to install Sandi's new dishwasher. She removes the access panel at the bottom of the new dishwasher so that we can get to all of the connection points.

21 Installing the new dishwasher should be easy. We'll attach the water supply line right here, ...

22 ... the drain hose right here ...

23 ... and make the electrical connections inside this box.

24 But before we do that we have to install a couple fittings, beginning here on the water supply lines. We're going to first wrap the fitting with Teflon tape, which is used to help make the plumbing seal tight.

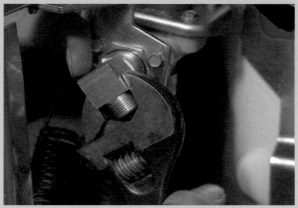

25 It acts as a lubricant helping the threads make better contact, thus preventing leaks. Without it you might get what plumbers call a false tight ...

26 ... where it feels tight but really it isn't.

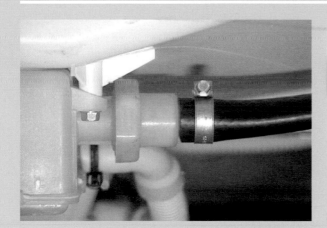

27 We're ready to install the drain line. With the dishwasher still out and away from the cabinet, it's easier to reach the drain hose, slip a clamp on the end and connect it. We slip the hose over the end of this fitting right here ...

28 ... tighten the clamp ...

29 ... and slide the dishwasher under the counter, making sure that we don't ruffle up the insulation that surrounds it.

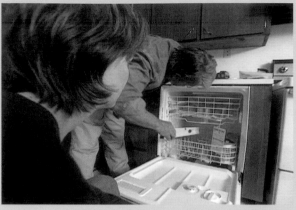

30 We check the dishwasher for level ...

31 ... and adjust as necessary by screwing the front feet in or out.

32 There are two mounting tabs at the top of the dishwasher. We use these to secure it to the bottom edge of the countertop.

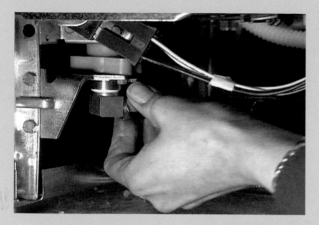

33 Back on the floor, Sandi reconnects the water supply line ...

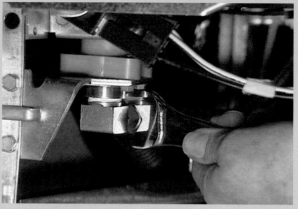

34 ... making sure the nut is wrenched tight.

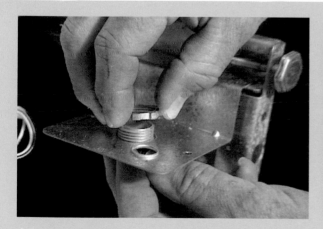

35 Next we're going to make our electrical connections inside this box. First we'll install what's called a strain relief.

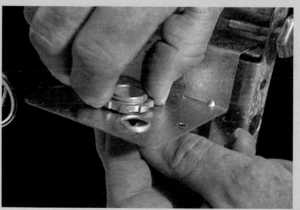

36 The strain relief helps prevent the wires from being accidentally pulled out of the box. First hand-tighten the nut, then snug it up with a pair of pliers.

37 The wires are pushed through the strain relief and into the box.

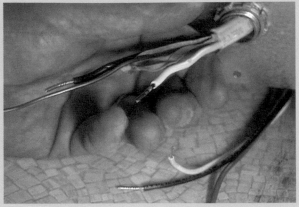

38 Next, we strip the insulation off the wires, leaving about one inch exposed ...

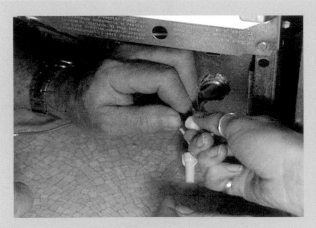

39 ... then connect them according to the manufacturer's instructions.

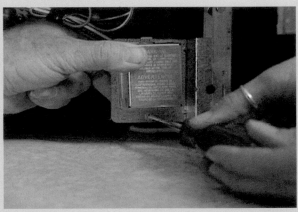

40 The last thing we do is replace the cover on the electrical box.

41 Now we can reinstall the access panel.

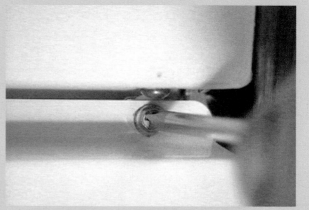

42 One last screw and then we can turn on the power and water.

43 We set a couple of switches and give it a test. It's working great and it's quiet — no rattles. While this is a fairly involved home improvement, it's well worth the time and effort.

Installing a Range Hood

MURPHY'S LAW SLOWS, BUT DOESN'T DERAIL, THIS KITCHEN-UPGRADE PROJECT

Ardina and Johnny Williams of Cooler, Georgia have asked for a house call. They want to install a kitchen exhaust fan and I'm going to see if I can help them.

1 Ardina shows me the kitchen, and while many range hood projects might be a replacement, this one is a start-from-scratch. She explains they've never had a range hood, and every time they turn on the stove it sets off the smoke detector.

2 Two things are required to install a range hood — electricity which we have — and a way to direct the exhaust to the outside. If we went up with the exhaust through the cabinets the exhaust pipe would be visible. Instead, we're going to go through the wall.

3 Johnny and Ardina start by checking to make sure there's enough space between the cabinets for the new range hood.

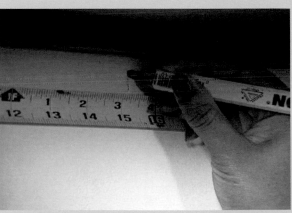

4 Then we find the center of the wall ...

211

5 ... and follow the manufacturers' detailed instructions to mark the position for the cutout.

6 This is what we're going to have to cut out — "X" marks the spot.

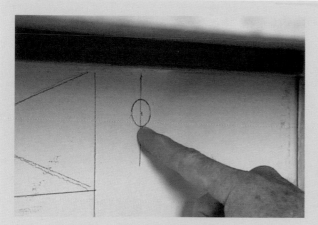

7 This is where the electrical wire will come through ...

8 ... and this is where the exhaust will go out. Of course these openings will also have to match up with these same openings in the back of the exhaust fan. Using a wallboard saw, Johnny cuts along the lines we've just drawn — until we hit a snag.

9 As is often the case with home improvement, the empty space we expected to find behind the wall is occupied by a copper water pipe. The only choice is to detour the pipe around the opening.

10 To do this, we remove the cabinet ...

11 ... and enlarge the opening in the wall.

12 While the wall is open, we take advantage of the easier access and drill a hole through the studding ...

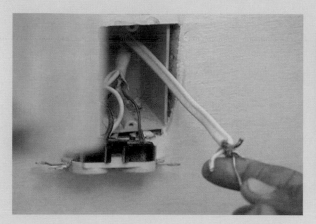

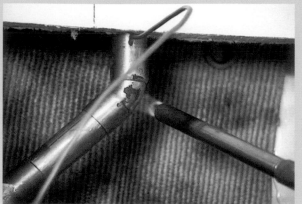

13 ... to run the new electrical wire for the range hood.

14 Then reroute and solder the copper pipe.

15 To close up the opening, we'll attach 1×3 cleats to the inside of the wall at the top and bottom ...

16 ... cut a piece of wallboard to fit ...

17 ... secure the new wallboard at these cleats ...

18 ... and patch the seams with joint tape and compound.

19 It was quite a detour, but we've gotten that pipe out of the way and right now we're looking at the back side of the exterior brick wall. To cut through, I'm going to bore four holes, one at each corner where we want the exterior hole to be.

20 We're using a carbide tipped bit and a hammer drill for this step. The drill hammers as it rotates, which will allow us to go through that brick a lot faster.

21 Johnny and I share the drilling duty. And before long, we have the corner holes bored out. For the outside, we drill a series of holes between the corners, perforating the outline of the opening.

22 Using a hammer and chisel, we remove the loose brick and mortar. We're going to start our installation right here on the outside by putting in a wall cap.

23 This is where the exhaust air will exit the building. Attached to the cap will be this short piece of duct that we cut down to length. It will slip up inside, and the entire unit will go through the wall.

24 Using sheet metal screws, I attach the duct to the wall cap.

25 Then seal the joint with duct tape.

26 A heavy bead of masonry adhesive will secure the cap to the brick wall and keep it sealed from wind and weather.

27 Once the duct has come through the wall, I use tin snips to cut the corners ...

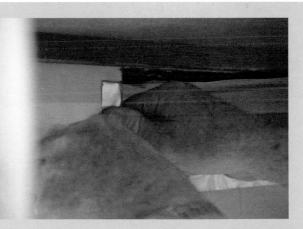

28 ... and bend the edges flush with the wall.

29 A flange around the duct makes a tight seal to the hood.

30 Because the underside of the cabinet is recessed, we'll need to install cleats to provide a mounting surface for the hood.

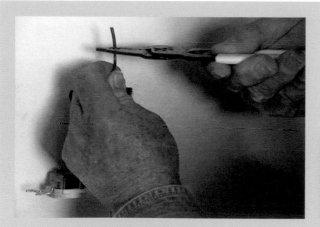

31 At the electrical outlet, I trim the insulation ...

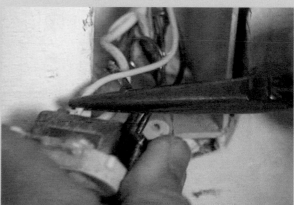

32 ... and make the connections for the wiring.

33 Finally we install four mounting screws to the cleats, driving them only half way in so we can slip the slotted mounting holes over the heads.

34 We slide the hood over the mounting screws, slide them into the permanent slot and fasten the screws.

35 Finally we connect the electrical wires to the hood, replace the access panel and snap the grease filter in place.

36 We decided a good test of the range hood would be a batch of burgers. The smell is making my mouth water, but the smoke alarm is silent. A successful project!

Installing a Tubular Skylight

A LIGHTING PROJECT THAT REQUIRES NO ELECTRICITY

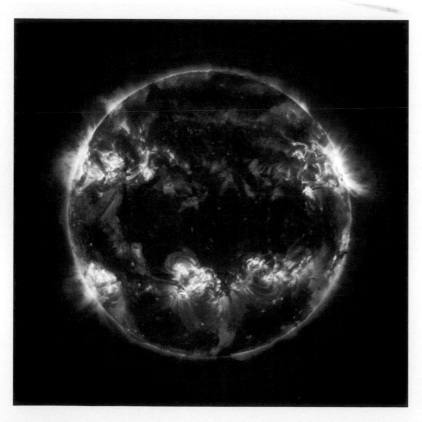

While it's not truly an electrical project, what better lighting project than not having to worry about wiring anything! Walk through the steps to harness the universe's natural light.

Photo Credit: TRACE Project, Stanford-Lockheed Institute for Space Research/NASA/Michael Benson, Kinetikon Pictures

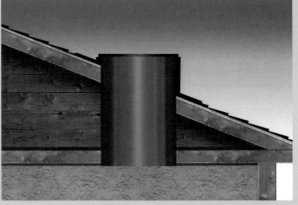

1 Jeannie and William Bragg's family room is comfortable, but it's quite a bit darker than the rest of the house. Our project is to install a tubular skylight that will help them lighten the room.

2 A tubular skylight consists of a light-weight reflective tube ...

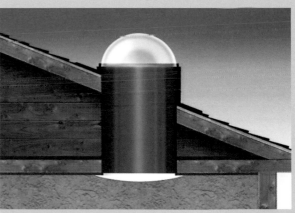

3 ... a roof dome ...

4 ... and ceiling diffuser.

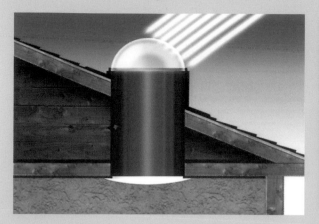

5 Sunlight enters the dome ...

6 ... is channeled down the reflective tubing ...

7 ... and enters the room through a diffuser ...

8 ... softly illuminating up to one-hundred square feet.

9 With a piece of masking tape, Jeannie marks her preferred location for the diffuser on the ceiling.

10 She uses a stud finder to locate the ceiling joists.

11 We're going to drop the tubular skylight between the ceiling joists. We don't want to be cutting those away, so our goal is to cut a fourteen-inch diameter hole in the ceiling, centered between the ceiling joists.

12 Jeannie begins by drilling an exploratory hole where we believe the centerpoint to be.

13 Then she inserts a coat hanger though the hole and into the attic.

14 From the attic, William locates the coat hanger and checks to make sure we're clear of the joists.

15 Then he positions a flashlight alongside the coat hanger and aims the beam up ...

16 ... to a clear spot between the rafters ...

17 ... which he marks.

18 Next he drills a hole through the roof ...

19 ... and leaves the bit protruding so it can be seen from the outside. Now, we have an unobstructed line from the roof, through the attic, and into the family room. The bit marks the centerpoint for the opening we'll be cutting in the roof.

20 This is the flashing that the skylight dome is going to attach to. We want it centered on the drill bit.

21   Once the flashing is in place, William takes a lumber crayon and draws a circle on the inside of the flashing, marking our opening. Now we're ready to cut a hole in their roof!

22   But before we start cutting, there's one thing I don't want to happen — have this cutout fall through and punch a hole in their ceiling. So, I'm showing William a little technique to prevent that. I drive a screw into the roof about three inches from our cut line.

23   By slipping the end of a pry bar over the screw head we've now got a handle that will allow us to keep a grip on the cutout.

24   Finally, the moment William has been anxiously anticipating. Using a reciprocating saw, I begin cutting a hole in the roof.

25 We finish up the cut. My pry bar trick works like a charm, allowing us to lift the circular cut-out out of the way.

26 Next we slip the reciprocating saw under the shingles and cut the roofing nails around the edge of the hole.

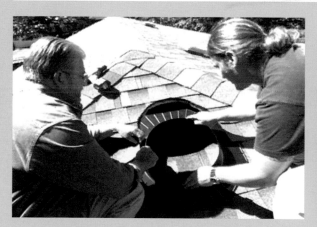

27 This will allow us to slip the flashing underneath the shingles.

28 We secure the flashing to the roof with some screws.

29 With the flashing in place we slip a section of reflective tube into the hole ...

30 ... until it seats against the top of the flashing.

31 We set the plastic roof dome in position ...

32 ... and secure it with a few screws.

33 Now it's time to cut a hole in the family room ceiling for the diffuser.

34 A drywall saw ...

35 ... gets the job done ...

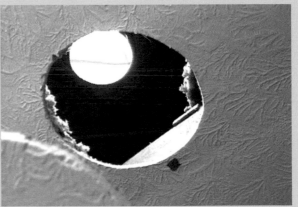

36 ... in a couple of minutes.

37 Our next step is to construct a long tube which is going to go up through the hole and connect to the piece that we put up on the roof.

38 It comes in sections. All we need to do is go ahead and hook the sections together.

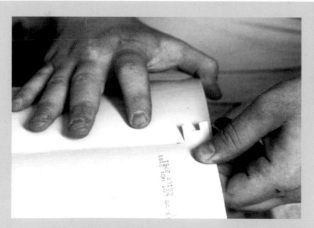

39 The sections go from flat, to tube, by connecting the tabs at the joints.

40 Now we apply aluminum tape over the joint to hold the sections together and prevent light from leaking out. The peel-and-stick backing makes the tape easy to use.

41 Burnishing or rubbing the tape with a cardboard roller insures a good seal.

42 We attach the tube section to the flange piece.

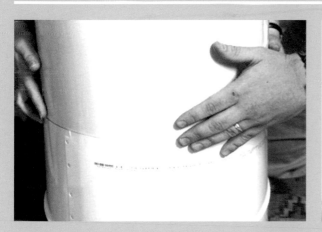

43 We assemble the tube sections by inserting one inside the other ...

44 ... and then taping the joints.

45 We slip in the next tube section ...

46 ... and Jeannie again tapes the joint.

47 Now the assembled sections are long enough to reach through the attic and connect to the flange piece in the roof.

48 The assembled sections are lifted through the ceiling hole, carefully aligned ...

49 ... and slipped over the roof section we installed earlier.

50 A flange on the bottom section is screwed into the ceiling.

51 The diffuser, which will soften the light, is snapped in place.

52 I can't believe the amount of light that's coming into the room. It really lightened up this whole corner of the room — and I didn't have to connect a wire!

Definitions

Alternating Current – A current that reverses at regular intervals of time with alternating positive and negative values. Type used in home electrical service.

Ampere (amp) – Unit of electrical current. Think of it as water flowing in a hose.

BX Cable – Metallic-sheathed cable containing A/C electrical wiring. Typically used when wiring would otherwise be exposed.

Circuit – A complete path over which an electric current can flow.

Circuit Breaker – A device designed to open and close a circuit. If an over current occurs, it will open the circuit automatically, protecting both the wiring and the appliance connected to that circuit. Circuit breakers can be reset.

Conduit – Tube that houses electrical wiring.

Current – The movement of electrons through a wire; measured in amperes.

Insulator – A device for fastening and supporting a conductor. Glass and porcelain are employed almost universally for supporting overhead wires.

Junction Box – Utility area where incoming current is connected in an electrical appliance.

Kilowatt – A unit of electrical power, equal to one thousands watts. See *watt*.

Meter – An electric indicating instrument as a voltmeter, ammeter, etc.

Negative – In electrical apparatus, the pole or direction toward which the current is suppose to flow.

Ohm – The unit of electrical resistance. See *resistance*.

Plug – A male electrical connector with contact prongs to connect mechanically and electrically to slots in the matching female socket.

Resistance – The opposition to the passage of an electric current. It converts electrical energy into heat.

Romex – Electrical wiring sheathed in a plastic coating.

Short Circuit – A fault in an electric circuit or apparatus. Usually caused by imperfect insulation, such that the current follows a by-path. In homes, this could possibly cause a fire unless the circuit is protected by a circuit breaker.

Switch – A device for making, breaking or changing the connections in an electric current.

Transformer – An apparatus used for changing the voltage and current of an alternating circuit.

Volt – The practical unit of electric pressure.

Wall Socket – Female electrical connectors that have slots or holes which accept and deliver current to the prongs of inserted plugs. Sockets are designed to accept only matching plugs and reject all others.

Watt – The practical unit of power or amount of electricity being used or consumed.

Wiring – Insulated conductors used to carry electricity.

Standard wire colors for flexible cable such as: extension cords, power (line) cords and lamp cords

COUNTRY	LIVE	NEUTRAL	PROTECTIVE EARTH/GROUND
EU, Australia & South Africa	brown	blue	green/yellow
Australia & New Zealand	brown	light blue	green/yellow
United States & Canada	black (brass)	white (silver)	green (green)

Standard wire colors for fixed cable in or behind walls

COUNTRY	LIVE	NEUTRAL	PROTECTIVE EARTH/GROUND
EU including UK	brown	blue	green & yellow
Australia & South Africa	red	black	green & yellow (core is usually bare and should be sleeved at terminations.)
United States & Canada	black, red, blue (brass)	white (silver)	green (green) or bare copper

Index

More great titles from Popular Woodworking and Betterway books!

THE COMPLETE GUIDE TO CONTRACTING YOUR OWN HOME

By Dave McGuerty & Kent Lester

This step-by-step guide to managing the construction of your own home is jamb packed with:

· To-do check lists for each phase of the construction process

· Hundreds of illustrations that clearly show what the author is teaching you

· Pages and pages of each necessary form you'll need to complete your home project

ISBN 13: 978-1-55870-465-7
ISBN 10: 1-55870-465-5
paperback, 320 p., #70378

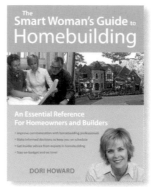

ISBN 13: 978-1-55870-817-4
ISBN 10: 1-55870-817-0
paperback, 160 p., #Z1027

THE SMART WOMAN'S GUIDE TO HOMEBUILDING

By Dori Howard

Using the information in this book, you can:

· Improve your communication with homebuilding professionals

· Make informed decisions to keep you on schedule

· Get insider advice from experts in homebuilding

· Stay on budget and on time!

POPULAR WOODWORKING'S ARTS & CRAFTS FURNITURE PROJECTS

This book offers a collection of twenty-five Arts & Crafts furniture projects for every room in your home. Some projects are accurate reproductions while others are loving adaptations of the style.

A bonus CD-ROM contains ten projects and ten technique articles to provide even more information on construction and finishing.

ISBN 13: 978-1-55870-846-4
ISBN 10: 1-55870-846-4
paperback, 128 p., #Z2115

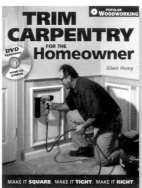

ISBN 13: 978-1-55870-814-3
ISBN 10: 1-55870-814-6
paperback with DVD, 128 p., #Z0953

TRIM CARPENTRY FOR THE HOMEOWNER

By Glen Huey

Master carpenter Glen Huey shows you:

· How to use ready-made supplies and materials from home center stores

· How to install or replace door, window, chair moulding and other room trims

· How to make and trim out fireplace surrounds and mantles

· How to install wainscotting and built-in furniture

These and other great woodworking books are available at your local bookstore, woodworking stores, or from online suppliers.

www.popularwoodworking.com